Movement Direction

Developing Physical Narrative for Performance

Performer Jordan Ajadi.

Movement Direction

Developing Physical Narrative for Performance

KATE FLATT

THE CROWOOD PRESS

First published in 2022 by
The Crowood Press Ltd
Ramsbury, Marlborough
Wiltshire SN8 2HR

enquiries@crowood.com

www.crowood.com

British Library Cataloguing-in-Publication Data
A catalogue record for this book is available from the British Library.

ISBN 978 0 7198 4060 9

Image credits
Alain de Chamberataud, page 151 (right); Annie Spratt, Unsplash, page 79; Annika Johansson, page 126;
Ardian Lumi, Unsplash, page 78; Asha Jennings-Grant, page 130 (bottom); Author's collection, pages 24,
45, 62, 66 (top), 74, 117; Chloe Lamford, page 65 (left); Chris Nash, pages 32, 39 (bottom), 58 (bottom), 87,
118; Engravings from *Rhetorical Gesture and Action* by Henry Siddons (1822). Royal Ballet School Special
Collections, pages 19 (bottom), 20 (left and right), 21 (left), 57 (top three), 61; Faisal Waheed, Unsplash,
page 66 (bottom); Hugh Hill, page 148 (left); Jack Thomson, cover and frontispiece, and pages 2, 12, 42,
47, 48 (all), 49 (all), 51 (all). 54 (top and bottom left), 88; Jacques Callot (1592–1635), *Balli di Sfessania*
(Tafelband), Potsdam 1921, Signatur: Wa 5604a, with kind permission of the Herzog August Bibliothek,
Wolfenbuettel, page 18 (all); Jake Weirick, Unsplash, page 105; Jemima Yong, page 129; Joe Hill-Gibbins,
pages 35 (all), 122, 123, 124, 125; Juan Miguel Agudo, Unsplash, page 65 (right); Karsten Winegeart,
Unsplash, page 96; Kristina Pulejkova, page 130 (top); Leandro de Carvalho, Unsplash, page 56 (top);
Ludovic des Cognets, pages 28, 39 (top), 54 (bottom right), 81, 136; Marie-Noëlle Robert, pages 109,
116; Márton Perlaki, page 152 (bottom right); Matthew Ball, page 73; Nikolas Louka, pages 26, 143; Oliver
Lamford, page 46; Peter Simpkin, page 155 (bottom right); Picryl, pages 76 (top and bottom), 93 (top and
bottom), 102; Pixabay, pages 57 (bottom), 99 (top); Ricardo Cruz, Unsplash, page 101; Ricardo Gomez
Angel, Unsplash, page 104; Robert Workman, pages 106, 114, 115, 120; Royal Central School of Speech
and Drama (photo by Ludovic des Cognets), pages 7, 71; Ruth Mulholland, page 149 (left); Shutterstock,
pages 17, 19 (top), 56 (bottom four), 82, 83, 89, 135; Steve Cummiskey, page 84; Thomas Bonometti,
Unsplash, page 99 (bottom); Tyler Nix, Unsplash, page 58 (top); Uta Scholl, Unsplash, page 16; Wasi
Daniju, page 31.

Typeset by Simon and Sons
Cover design by Blue Sunflower Creative
Printed and bound in India by Parksons Graphics

CONTENTS

ACKNOWLEDGEMENTS

CONTRIBUTORS

Heartfelt thanks to all the movement directors and directors, who gave of their time for interviews and approving transcripts of the conversations. Their contributions enrich this book with the varied and enlivening accounts of their views and practice. The case studies include Vicki Amedume, Lucy Cullingford, Sarah Fahie, Jonathan Goddard, Joyce Henderson, Steven Hoggett, Jos Houben, Asha Jennings-Grant, Cameron McMillan, Ingrid Mackinnon, Diane Alison Mitchell, Sacha Milevic Davies, Anna Morrissey, Jenny Ogilvie, Ita O'Brien and Ayse Tashkiran.

I am also very grateful for rich, informative conversations held with a wider group and how that has helped shape the scope and detail of the book. These include movement director Natasha Harrison and directors David Lan, Femi Elufowoju Jr, Brigid Larmour and Matt Ryan.

ILLUSTRATIONS

I am grateful to the photographers who have granted me permission to use their work.

These include Robert Workman, Matthew Ball, Stephen Cummiskey, Chris Nash, Joe Hill-Gibbins, Chloe Lamford, Oliver Lamford and Barbara Stott. Special thanks to Jack Thomson for the cover image and also performer Jordan Ajadi for their continuing collaboration.

Images by Ludovic des Cognets are from a RCSSD Master Class, given in 2009.

Workshop participants, former students at RCSSD, also gave their permission and they include Vicky Aracas, Daphna Attias, Zoë Cob, Brad Cook, Claire Dunn, Anna Healey, Filippos Kanakaris and Terry O'Donovan.

Many thanks to the Herzog August Bibliothek, Wolfenbuettel, Germany, for permission for the *commedia dell'arte* images in Chapter 1. Grateful thanks also to Anna Meadmore at The Royal Ballet School Special Collections for use of the images from *Rhetorical Gesture and Action; Adapted to the English Drama* by Henry Siddons (1822), a text that belonged to Dame Ninette de Valois, donated to the library in 1963.

THANKS

Special thanks go to Ayse Tashkiran, movement director and educator for her support and insight, in reading and commenting on aspects of this book.

Heartfelt appreciation and admiration for the many performers, actors and movement artists from diverse backgrounds, whose talent and investigation into movement and embodiment feeds into and carries the work of movement directors everywhere.

On a personal level, I am deeply grateful for the support, love, insight and patience of my husband Tim Lamford, especially for his care of our family, when they were growing up, and whilst I was away from home working as a movement director. Without him this book would not have been written.

OPPOSITE: **Actors in a movement class at the Royal Central School of Speech and Drama.**

INTRODUCTION

Life requires movement.

Aristotle

IN THIS BOOK

This book is about what movement direction entails and introduces the multi-faceted craft of the movement director, along with the knowledge, skills of invention, research and creative vision that the role encompasses.

Professional Practitioners

In the preparation of this book, I have drawn on my own experiences of working in theatre on plays, opera and musicals as a movement director and theatre choreographer. I have also been grateful for conversations and interviews with movement directors who are practitioners active in the field. This has resulted in contributions and accounts of their practice, which appear as examples, quotes and case studies relating to shows and productions they have created. These movement experts have generously offered accounts of how their ideas are realized through approaches to research, studio strategies, script study and collaboration as part of the challenge and creative problem-solving of the movement director's practice. The chapters offer insight into working in the professional context, the expressive body, the actor's process and approaches to working with scripts on plays and in the world of opera. Also introduced briefly are examples of applied skills in the context of motion capture, physical comedy, fashion shoots, contemporary circus and intimacy co-ordination in film and television. The final chapter on collaboration includes views, observations and conversations with directors on this important aspect of how movement direction in live theatre occurs.

MOVEMENT MEMORIES

The power of communication in the theatre can create a vivid, lasting memory through movement. Seeing live performance across decades has shown me how movement speaks without the need for words. These few recalled moments remind me that, by simple but imaginative means, movement leaves a resonant impression. Common to these memories are great performers, whose imagination, precision of rhythm, bodily detail and the connection to the space around them leaves an indelible imprint.

Marcel Marceau in Performance

The great mime artist Marcel Marceau performed a programme of vignettes that peopled the stage with characters who communicated volumes without words. He transformed the space by his action, playing every character himself. His skill was in communicating character detail through his masterful use of an expressive body. His gift was a precise yet playful approach that awakened the imagination of the audience, leaving an indelible image. Here are two examples from his repertoire of vignettes:

- The Tribunal
  Marceau became an elderly and rather doddery judge. I recall that he walked up three steps to

a podium and tripped on the top step, before then presiding over the court. This was all played on a flat stage floor, with no props or scenery. He went on to play, alternately, the prosecutor and the criminal on trial in the courtroom.

- The Mask

  Marceau was playing with two imaginary, archetypal masks of comedy and tragedy, switching back and forth between them, at times quite rapidly. In this game, the comic mask eventually became stuck on his face. All attempts to remove it were in vain; his body then portrayed the limp despair of being trapped, seemingly without escape, but with an insane, fixed grin stuck on his face.

The Tempest (1610–11) directed by Giorgio Strehler, Piccolo Theatre, Milan (1978)

I saw the famous Piccolo Theatre production of Shakespeare's *The Tempest* at the Los Angeles Olympic Arts Festival in 1984. Directed by visionary Giorgio Strehler and played in Italian, I was able to understand the whole of the play without knowing it well, nor much Italian. He used theatre magic and movement with great dexterity to create the world of the play.

The movement elements for the storm at the start of the play consisted of a stage full of quantities of billowing silk manipulated by a company of invisible people situated below the platform of the simple, wooden set. Instantly there was emphasis on movement and rhythm coming from the performers. I have never forgotten Aerial's arrival. A slender, androgynous performer in a costume resembling a cloud of white silk descended from above. Suspended on a wire, the air spirit greeted Prospero in a high-pitched, bird-like voice. The movement involved tumbling, rising and falling on a vertical wire, assisted by an unseen operator. At one point, Prospero's arms were outstretched and, for a fleeting moment, Aerial balanced on tiptoe, alighting on his hand before flying upward again. It was a magical revelation of what movement can do to embody the air spirit that is Aerial. Any YouTube clips available do not do justice to the lightness of the performer and their sense of flight.

Leonide Massine in Rehearsal

Massine was working on a revival of his *Le Beau Danube* in 1972 with Joffrey Ballet. One rehearsal day, he became exasperated with the young dancer playing the hussar (Massine's own role). The dancer, who was very able with all the danced material, could not seem to embody the thought behind a particular moment and the focus required in the action. Standing, centre stage, he was asked to slowly raise his arm and then give a flourish as if the opening phrases of the *Blue Danube Waltz* made him remember something. Massine, then seventy-six years old, lost patience. He got up from his chair, went to the centre of the room and showed what he wanted from the moment. His energy from the spine and the gesture initiated from his centred torso radiated outward into the space, whilst the ensemble couples waltzed slowly around him to the slow, dream-like strains of Strauss' *Blue Danube Waltz*. The years rolled away, to reveal a young man recalling a romance.

MY OWN JOURNEY INTO MOVEMENT DIRECTION

I became a movement director before I fully understood what the term meant. I had originally trained as a dancer in ballet and contemporary dance. I had studied choreography with Leonide Massine, t'ai chi ch'üan and the Alexander technique. I also travelled extensively in Eastern Europe learning, watching and researching traditional folk dance in ritual and village settings. I began choreographing seriously, after early beginnings, in my mid-twenties. After developing my own sole-authored projects, I was asked to work on the opera *Eugene Onegin* by Tchaikovsky, and immediately felt at home in that world. Four years later, after a clutch of other operas, and following the arrival of two children, I was phoned about a 'new musical'. The director, Trevor Nunn, explained what might be required. I suggested naively that he might be looking for a kind of 'invisible choreography'. The term movement director did not widely exist in 1985. I accepted the creative challenge to work on the original *Les Misérables* at the RSC on the hunch of 'a funny feeling I should do this'. After discussing with my husband, a fellow creative artist in dance, we agreed that it might be hard with our two small children to manage at this time, but an important step. Who knew what the future held? I decamped to a flat in the Barbican with the children and engaged a nanny whilst my husband went on a UK tour with his company Spiral Dance. I started rehearsals at the RSC in their Barbican studios finding myself in a world of storytelling, movement, bodies and the characters of the now famous, epic, musical story.

A Voyage of Discovery

The creative process began with rehearsal days full of exploration and improvisation to discover the ensemble language and the way that the many stories within *Les Misérables* could be told through action. The work also encompassed the development of many individual characters, some only appearing for a few moments, others growing, changing, living and dying in the world of Victor Hugo's novel. After ten days, out of an eight-week rehearsal period, together with the directors John Caird and Trevor Nunn, we began on the task of staging the story, aided by the famous revolving stage, of this epic novel.

The rehearsal process revealed that, although experienced as a choreographer, I had entered a new and rather different role. I led a daily warm-up, created frameworks for improvisation as movement and body work for the actors, whereby many

LES MISÉRABLES, DIRECTED BY TREVOR NUNN AND JOHN CAIRD, RSC (1985)

The embodiment of anger in the musical number *At the End of the Day* was a key moment of creative endeavour and realization. I offered an observation, 'If you're angry, it's so hard to move'. 'Can you make an improvisation for that?' was the response. Next morning, following overnight planning, struggles with my five-year-old daughter missing her father and five-month-old son not too keen to sleep through, I made a start.

For the improvisation, I asked the actors to recall a sporting action then to physicalize it, locating the energy of the action, and where the impulse points for the movement were in the body. There was quickly a room full of action: footballers, tennis aces, cricketers and javelin throwers. On an impulse, I asked them to capture the energy of the action, focus on the point of maximum impact (as in kick or hit of the ball) and stop, and not follow through the action. This meant capturing all the force within the now still body and suspending the action. 'What is supposed to happen?' asked an actor. 'I don't know [I really didn't] but try it and let's find out?'

Forces and Gestures

The body shapes that emerged were full of contained force. The actors went on to add gestures associated with anger – a clenched fist, a pointed finger of accusation, two hands showing empty frustration or rage. Often the gestures needed to be pulled in toward the body, at other times they spilled outwards or upwards.

Interestingly, the force of the action went down the body, into the ground and outward into gesture. This contributed to the expression of the powerful lyrics, telling the frustration of a group of able-bodied people, with no work, angry at factory owners. With bursts of action, propelled forward and yet held back, they travelled on a straight line, arriving downstage, with the final words confronting the audience with an accusation, full of embodied anger. With this physicality, the words landed with force and clarity.

characters and scenes emerged. I drew on my earlier studies with Massine, especially his work on the skeleton, as well as finding a sense of weight and rhythm, which gave me extremely valuable tools to explore with. Energy, emotion and different bodily states were explored and from these were developed the musical numbers. The movement improvisation tasks helped the actors find and create the undernourished bodies of beggars, the physicality of toffs, the body stories of whores and the many other characters whose powerful emotions told Victor Hugo's epic story for the musical it was to become.

FURTHER MOVEMENT ADVENTURES

Following on from the adventure that *Les Misérables* became, I took up opportunities as a movement director over the next few decades on some extraordinary new productions with wonderful performers who have all taught me so much. The source material, scripts, songs and libretti that I have had the privilege to research, prepare and create within, have been life-changing in terms of ideas and the journeys I have undertaken alongside performers and directors. With that comes an affirmation that a simple hunch, as a sketched idea, can grow to become a powerful movement sequence within the world of a play. The bodies of the performers and their actions are a vital part of how a story is communicated to an audience. I have also been fortunate to have had a ringside seat to witness the work of exceptional directors and to participate with them in the development of beautiful moments of live theatre. My work, as provider of movement for productions of theatre, opera and musicals, has reaped rewards and memories that I will always cherish.

Trial and Error

Looking back to the beginning of a career of making theatre, there have been some tricky challenges. There is potential for a developing idea to not land properly, to be misunderstood or to just go wrong in the rehearsal context. This risk is always present in creative enterprise where trial and error are at the centre of creative endeavour. Occasionally, performers feel insecure or are unable to envisage how movement observations and guidance offered can help them. Aside from that, there are many pleasures and discoveries to be found in how moments come alive through the performers and how they offer expressive meaning for an audience. Despite the best of intentions, collaborative engagement with directors can entail difference in taste, opinions, ego and, at times, misunderstandings or even friction. The movement director needs to become open and a skilled, alert navigator, offering ideas and material, guiding and shaping within the flow of creative action. When this goes well, it is possible to break new ground and find new approaches and pathways.

Embracing the New

Movement direction as a career involves discovery, growth and being prepared to try new things and inspiring other people to do so with you. It can also mean stepping out of a comfort zone into a new place. It is important to remain grounded and at times to be somewhat fearless. In the maelstrom of production rehearsals and the hub of creativity, managing confidence and fear of the unknown really counts. I stand by this wonderful observation from the late, great, education theorist Sir Ken Robinson:

> *...if you're not prepared to be wrong, you'll never come up with anything original...*
> Ken Robinson and Lou Aronica, The Element:
> How Finding Your Passion Changes Everything
> (Penguin Books, 2009)

CHAPTER 1

WHAT IS MOVEMENT DIRECTION?

Movement directors work with the physical, living bodies at the heart of a theatre production. They are called upon to create a movement language or physical style or to manifest – through performing bodies – the more enigmatic, elusive or otherwise absent parts of a theatre text.

Ayse Tashkiran, Movement Directors in Contemporary Theatre *(Methuen, 2020)*

MOVEMENT DIRECTION

Movement direction in contemporary theatre production is increasingly recognized and valued as a significant component of all the elements that make up live theatre performance. Movement work is developed to be subtly expressive in the body of a performer or more visible as distinct sequences and fluid transitions in ensemble creation. These can reflect reality as believable narrative serving to strengthen and delineate the world of a play or opera or offer heightened action by more abstract means.

Movement direction can involve all the following:

- Research into the source of movement and action in the script or libretto.
- Staging ensemble work as group or choral expression.
- Making movement components for scene changes in a production.
- Creation of movement 'scape' as physicality in the world of a play or opera.
- Creating a historical style in movement for a given context.
- Working with an audio environment, which may include music.
- Developing and enriching character in an actor's performance.
- Working with dance forms.

THE MOVEMENT DIRECTOR'S ROLE

The movement director is engaged to develop, arrange, oversee and coach material on all aspects of movement activity for stage presentation. They operate in collaboration, in ways that their creativity and knowledge are visible within the envelope of a director's overall concept. The authorship of a movement director becomes apparent in the physicality, action, body language and characterization carried by the performers. Movement directors collaborate, observe and accompany the performer's process in the arena of the studio, where invention, chemistry and intuitive responses are all at play. The movement director's role in working with performers can broadly entail all or some of the following:

- Knowledge and insight about the body as instrument of expression.
- Support and skill development as training for performers.
- Leading a warm-up for an ensemble at the start of the rehearsal day.
- Coaching dance skills for social and historical dances.

OPPOSITE: **Performer Jordan Ajadi in rehearsal.**

WHAT DO MOVEMENT DIRECTORS SAY?

The movement director's art and skill are probably best defined in the words of professional practitioners who work in a range of settings.

Steven Hoggett

A movement director is responsible for anything that moves on the stage with an inherent quality. This could be the performers, a piece of furniture, or an object that is flying through the air. The role means creatively engaging with three distinct aspects of theatre-making:

- *Creating sequences – often to music or soundscape but without text.*
- *Character development – through bodily expression and physicality.*
- *Scene changes – as transitions within an unfolding narrative.*

Lucy Cullingford

A movement director views the play through a physical lens; moves bodies, words, time and space from the functional into the epic world; navigates emotion into the physical realm expanding the character's inner life before the audience.

Sasha Milevic Davies

Movement direction is about working with the body in action and along with that, the rhythm and spatial qualities of that action. It is incredibly important that the pacing of the action, not only is integral, but also has an influence on the world of words. It involves collaborative decisions with the director and with a team who are together creating a visual, as well as a narrative, world in the staging of a play with sophisticated use of technology, lighting and design.

- Enabling the body and imagination to connect.
- Observing how psychological states and thoughts of a specific character are expressed, embodied and perceived by the audience.
- Enabling embodied emotion to be legible and believable in characterization.
- Drawing on skills, techniques and insights drawn from diverse movement traditions.
- Clarity in communication toward a collaborative outcome.
- Problem-solving.

Movement Director or Choreographer?

There is some debate around the similarities between the two roles. The term choreographer first emerged early in the twentieth century. The term movement director is possibly newer, although the practice is undoubtedly older. A variety of terms for movement, choreography or dance can be found in the list of creatives on a production. They include movement director, director of movement, movement by, dance director, musical staging, dance arrangement or choreography.

Similar Skills

There are inevitably crossover areas with similar skills being employed. Both practitioners organize movement, dance material and action by solving problems imaginatively and often at speed. As practitioners they may share an approach, and working methods may be similar, but the purpose behind the outcomes can be very different. Here is an outline of the two roles to help unpack the approaches to creating:

A movement director:

- Is trained and experienced with movement skills.
- Uses skill and craft to author a vision specifically for the movement world of a production.
- Creates with performers from a range of disciplines.
- Develops their work alongside the director's vision for a production.
- Is concerned with defining a physicality relevant to, or drawn from, a script.
- Can create or arrange sequences drawn from dance forms, with an integrated purpose.
- Is concerned with embodied emotion, thought and intention of performers.
- Works on legibility of movement in space and time.

A choreographer:

- Is trained and experienced in dance technique and movement skills.
- Creates dance as abstract, thematic or narrative material.
- Is sole author, in terms of material, vision and concept for a choreographic work or ballet.
- Uses the facility and skills of trained dancers rather than actors, singers or other performers.
- Articulates meaning through shaping dance in space and time.
- Creates to music, as in dance numbers in musicals or featured dance interludes in opera.
- A theatre choreographer collaborates with a director to provide choreography to a brief.

Recognition of the Craft

The creative outcomes perceived as movement direction may or may not be recognized by critics, venues, producers and possibly audiences. A debate hovers around the fact that movement direction, when skilfully deployed, becomes fully and seamlessly integrated into the whole and does not always stand out as a separate entity from the rest of the production. The movement element of a performance contributes to enhanced storytelling, characterization that engages with the actor's process in the rehearsal room and to the work of the director who provides the framework or envelope for the production. Choreographic authorship is more easily recognizable as a separate entity and may employ dancers' facility, appearing as dance with music, within a work.

WORKING METHODS

Living Material

The medium of human movement, by its very nature, is central to the expressive art of communication. As a living, slippery, changeable material, it is distilled in live theatre as embodiment of character, behaviour and underlying thought, which the performer expresses. There are diverse activities involved in working with movement that are unpacked across the course of the following chapters. Embodied knowledge and a discerning eye are significant aspects of the skill set needed by practitioners working in the field. The studio and stage demand of the movement director that they have done their research, as well as offering immediacy and sure-footed instincts in the handling of performers, ideas and imagination. Their work, integrated and subsumed into the whole of what an audience experiences, undeniably contributes to making a production distinctive as a theatre performance.

Working with Actors

Movement directors work in relation to the actor's process, collaborating on movement, observing and feeding-back in terms of how the physicality is perceived in the context of a scene. In creating movement action, the heart of 'why' and with 'what intention' within the movement will emerge in relation to the director's vision. The actor's process is about finding out and synthesizing information to make offers of movement from the centrality of all the other information they are carrying about the character. The answer to the question 'Why do I move?' is something

Epidaurus Theatre, Greece.

the actor needs to discover organically, rather than have imposed upon them. In this way the movement director acts as a provocateur or catalyst to action. If formal technical instruction is involved, it needs to be clarified to the actor as such, so that it becomes part of a palette of resources for them to draw on.

THEATRE MOVEMENT TRADITIONS – A BRIEF INTRODUCTION

Theatre is an ancient art and the use of movement within it a vital and ideally integrated component. These few introduced here, out of the many theatre traditions from across the globe, can be investigated through wider reading. They have developed in different eras in different parts of the world and show that movement is at the heart of a work and that a performer's skill is integral to the form.

> *She waved her arms and sketched in the air an image of a soundless voice, speaking with hands and moving eyes in a graphic picture of silence full of meaning.*
>
> Polyhymnia, the Greek muse of rhetoric and hymns, described in the Dionysiaca of Nonnus from c. 400 BC

Ancient Greek Theatre

The world of expressive bodily movement is as ancient and archetypal as the expressive art of song and the ancient charcoal drawings found on the walls of darkened caves. As was known to the Classical Greek and Roman orators, movement of the performer, along with voice and emotion, is integral to the delivery of meaning. The Greeks named nine muses as their attributes of artistic expression, and at least three of them are associated with movement and the rhetorical gestures used to accompany oration.

Ancient Greek theatre is a tradition with no material surviving that can confidently be said to belong to the form. Theatre performances took place at open-air festivals in honour of the gods. They were played on an open stage, called an *orchestra*, with a wide, stepped, almost circular arena for the audience. Performers wore masks covering their faces, requiring them to act with the whole body. This would have been physically demanding and require the use of movement and muscular tension to convey emotions, which in modern theatre or film we see in the faces of actors.

> *Movement... involved dances normally in a formation either on a rectangular or circular basis and while it might occasionally become*

Movement of a choral group, portrayed on a Greek vase.

wild and rapid, it was usually solemn and decorous, a style sometimes called emmeleia... *literally harmony.*

Oliver Taplin, Greek Tragedy in Action
(Routledge, 1993)

A chorus of fifteen male performers provided singing and dancing in a series of sequences throughout a play. These provided commentary on the interaction of the characters and praised the gods. The idea of integrating an ensemble of expressive, moving bodies to tell stories has its descendants in opera with a singing chorus, in ensembles for musical theatre and in ballet with a *corps de ballet* of dancers.

Commedia dell'Arte

The legacy of this form of improvised theatre, which flourished in Renaissance Italy, is important for its characters, influence on performance skills, use of half masks and improvisation. Illustrations from 1700 in Giorgio Lambranzi's *New and Curious School of Theatrical Dancing* (Dover Edition, 2002) give an impression of *commedia dell'arte* scenes in theatre performance. The form was known to Shakespeare, used by Molière in his plays and influenced the *buffo* or comic characters in Mozart's *Marriage of Figaro*. Significant aspects have been documented,

used in training systems and influenced the work of masters Vsevelod Meyerhold, Georgio Strehler, Jacques Lecoq and the choreographer Leonide Massine.

There is no single name that we can attach as originator of the form, yet it is understood as having had a significant element of vibrant, movement characterization at its heart. Professional players in Italy and beyond formed travelling troupes and developed skilful comedic techniques for outdoor performances in the street, square or courtyard, as well as in theatres. There were set scenarios that relied on the wit and playful movement detail of the performers for the plots involving recognizable, known characters. The performers' skills included mask work, dance, singing, comic routines and acrobatic skills, with a well-developed movement language of character work that was recognizable and apparent through gait, differing rhythms and behaviour. The characters included servants, known as *zanni*, lovers, clowns, braggarts and fighters, along with the roles of Harlequin, Columbine, Pantalone, Pulcinella and Scaramouche.

Kabuki Theatre

Japanese Kabuki theatre is a distinctive theatre tradition that is highly theatrical with elaborate

Cap. Mala Gamba.   Cap. Bellauita.

Cap. Bonbardon.   Cap. Grillo.

Pasquariello Truonno.   Meo Squaquara.

Commedia dell'arte characters.

costumes, make up, wigs and weaponry. Action of the performers includes distinctive stylization in the vocal work and movement. The performances are actor-centred, rather than led by a director, and the plots, usually in one act, tell stories in a way that subordinates the literary aspect in favour of theatrical effectiveness, often to suit a particular actor.

Kabuki can be translated as comprising 'dance-sing-skill'. The actors work with *mie*, translated as 'rhymes we say'. The movement material and its inclusion show a refined form developed over years of study and apprenticeship. The movement in performance follows a pattern offering a sequence of activity that arrives at a significant tableau. Kabuki movement, though fluid and graceful, is characteristic in how, with increasingly rhythmic movement, the performer achieves a place of equilibrium, or attitude, as a significant static moment, which ranges from semi-realistic to bizarre or grotesque. Neither movement nor timing aims to be realistic but the essential quality in the movement is that of a balanced, sculptural tension.

The theatre layout is like Western theatres, with the significant feature of the *hanimichi*, a long, raised promenade platform connecting stage right with the entrance to the auditorium. The actors enter and leave by this, and play important scenes here, bringing them close to the audience, seated around and just below them. The actor is accompanied by the presence of a shadowy figure, a *kurogo*, dressed entirely in black, which in Japanese theatre tradition makes him invisible to the audience. The role is as a kind of servant to the action for help with costumes and props. Kabuki is intrinsically stylized and rich in showmanship for which the actors train through a long apprenticeship to attain their craft. The best-known role type is that of *onnagata* or female impersonation, where male actors who specialize in this, play young, middle-aged or old women. Male roles are the handsome man, the lord, the superhero, as well as clerks, villains and comic roles.

Elizabethan and Early Modern Theatre

Elizabethan theatre placed importance on rhetorical gesture, which has a connection with the art of expressive oratory from ancient times. The use of movement as gesture is documented in the writing of John Bulwer (1644) and in his book *Chirologia*, it is described as having 'the art of manuall rhetoricke, consisting of the naturall expressions, digested by art in the hand, as the chiefest instrument of eloquence'. Bulwer outlines advice for actors and

Kabuki drama.

orators with a significant distinction made between natural expression and rhetorical action.

Shakespeare

We can't go back to see what was done in the performance of his plays, but it is probable that Shakespeare considered movement a significant part of the actor's expression. In *Hamlet*, Ophelia describes Hamlet's actions in precise detail to her father Polonius (Act II, Scene 1). Her description of their encounter, and his odd behaviour toward her, suggests he is not of sound mind. Hamlet then tells the players who have arrived to perform at Elsinore, to 'Suit the action to the word, the word to the action' (Act III, Scene 2). He continues to show interest in the quality of movement and language in the players' delivery. He seems to be suggesting, as an aspirant director, not to overact or play the emotions too powerfully.

> **...** *nor do not saw the air too much with your hand, thus, but use all gently; for in the very torrent, tempest, and, as I may say, the whirlwind of passion, you must acquire and beget a temperance that may give it smoothness... pray you, avoid it.*
>
> *(Act II, Scene 2).*

Henry Siddons

If we fast-forward a hundred years from Bulwer's writing to developments of modern theatre, the emphasis on gestural codes, demeanour and behaviour as rhetorical action is noted by the celebrated actor and theatre manager Henry Siddons

Doubt.

Vulgar astonishment.

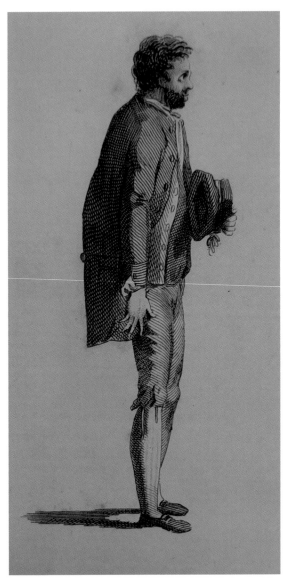

Rustic cunning.

(1741–1815). Practical illustrations are given in *Rhetorical Gesture and Action; Adapted to the English Drama* by Henry Siddons (1822). These sixty-five engravings, published after Siddons' death, indicate the range and scope of his observations of performers and the portrayal of intentions through gesture and physicality. Siddons' intriguing work is an interpretation of an earlier book from 1785, by German theatre director Johann Jakob Engel.

Six Viewpoints

The Six Viewpoints were conceived by postmodern choreographer Mary Overlie (1946–2020) and have been a significant development in American twentieth-century theatre practice. Overlie's work was furthered through Anne Bogart and Tina Landau's practice and writing. Tina Landau is a director and ensemble member of Steppenwolf Theatre Company based in Chicago. Anne Bogart references the Viewpoints for training and exploration

Obsequiousness.

The authors suggest that the Viewpoints are a timeless system:

> ... *belonging to the natural principles of movement, time, and space. We have simply articulated a set of names for things that already exist, things that we do naturally and have always done, with greater or lesser degrees of consciousness and emphasis. [The Viewpoints offer] a philosophy, translated into a technique for training performers, building ensembles, and creating movement for the stage.*
>
> The Viewpoints Book: A Practical Guide to
> Viewpoints and Composition
> *(Landau and Bogart, 2006, ch. 2)*

Contemporary Devised Theatre

In contemporary devised theatre, movement forms an integral part of the development of new work, co-created during the rehearsal process by the team of performers with diverse skills, drawn together by a director. During this time, there may be no preexisting text or scripted material. The historic precedent of devised theatre practice can be seen in *commedia dell'arte*, where known plots, themes and scenarios act as a framework enabling improvisation by the performers. The work is configured, according

in her work with the SITI company, which she co-founded in New York with Japanese director Tadashi Suzuki in 1992. Now a professor at Columbia University, she leads their Graduate Theatre Concentration. The approach of Suzuki and the Six Viewpoints are widely, and confidently, used in actor and performer training in the USA. The Viewpoints or SSTEMS are outlined as Space, Story, Time, Emotion, Movement and Shape. Bogart and Landau expanded and developed the Viewpoints to represent not only approaches to movement for the performer and tools as physical techniques but as a lens through which to observe and direct action. Their work offers, beyond the physical, a philosophical and aesthetic dimension in the creative act of making and developing new theatre.

Step Ladder and a Goat, a devised production at Imagine Watford Festival 2016. The performers are Amir Giles, Finn Cooke and JD Broussé.

to the specialist talents and skills of the performers and the subject matter, and the company may work as a collective, with no hierarchy in the organizational structure. The resultant performance, as an entity, is made through play, exploration with the elements, skill sharing and improvisation. In this mode of theatre-making, the movement director is present to create, engineer and imagine physical action with groups and individual actors, all bringing movement to life. The movement director's role requires not only the craft and observations of their own discipline, but also understanding, empathy, respect and participation of a shared vision toward the outcomes in performance and its presentation to the audience. Devised theatre is found, to name only a few examples from the UK, in the work of Theatre de Complicité, Kneehigh Theatre and Frantic Assembly.

KEY PIONEERS

The work of the contemporary movement director stands on the shoulders of pioneers in the art of movement. These few, introduced here, have developed the art form through schemes and systems for the study of movement for theatre. Their discoveries, briefly outlined, offer significant frameworks of understanding in a wide field of bodily knowledge that has had influence on training practices for performers in the use of movement, as opposed to dance, for theatre (see Further Reading).

Francois Delsarte (1811–71)

Francois Delsarte was a pioneer in understanding movement and rhetorical gesture. Delsarte coached orators and actors, amongst others, in the bodily expression of emotions. His interest was to create a connection between inner emotional experience and the use of gesture. He examined how the breath, movement dynamics and voice could encompass expression in the body, and identified principles in practice for expressive communication, long before there was something called movement direction. He did not write about his work, but the quote below is taken from writing by one of his pupils, who was part of the development of Delsarte's teachings in the USA, through the interest of Steele Mackay and Genevieve Stebbins. Through them, his work became the foundation of a system of teaching and training in physical culture. It also influenced the early American Modern Dance pioneers, including Ruth St. Denis and Ted Shawn. Delsarte's importance is that he is credited with drawing attention to much older observations from Ancient Greece and the Renaissance.

The body becomes alive to the feeling within, and the soul awakens. The mind first grasps an idea, which is then conveyed to the thought or emotion within. All action should radiate from the center. The body is swayed according to the strength of the emotion, until the latter, seeking a wider outlet, flows into the extremities and becomes a gesture – the only true gesture.... Gesture too frequently becomes a meaningless wave of the arm, devoid of all feeling, while the speaker's body and lower limbs might be carved from wood or stone, so little expression is displayed in either.

Eleanor Georgen, The Delsarte System of Physical Culture *(Butterick Publishing Co., 1893)*

Delsarte's approach and methods, as developed in America in the early twentieth century by his followers, included elements summarized here, which are all found, although perhaps differently named, in contemporary actor movement training. Referred to in 'Delsarte Heritage' by Nancy Lee Chalfa Ruyter, they are outlined as:

- Relaxation exercises (sometimes including falls).
- Posture work and harmonic poise.
- Work on breath.
- Walking, leg attitudes, exercises for freedom of joints and spine.
- Spiral successional movements.
- Attitudes of expression.
- Performance forms.

Nancy Lee Chalfa Ruyter, 'Delsarte Heritage', The Journal of the Society for Dance Research, *Vol. 14, No. 1 (Summer, 1996), pp. 62–74*

Vsevelod Meyerhold (1874–1940)

Meyerhold was a Russian director and actor whose ground-breaking experiments in the 1920s into non-realistic, heightened action made him a pioneer of modern theatre. He developed radical ideas for non-representational theatre in his symbolist productions. He rebelled against the naturalism of Stanislavsky's art theatre and developed his innovative practice known as 'biomechanics' in which his actors behaved in puppet-like, mechanistic ways. Biomechanics used by Meyerhold, developed as an acting system that used motion rather than language. Actors were coached with emphasis on bodily action, gymnastics and acrobatics, and often performed on a bare, harshly lit stage using scaffoldings, ladders and ramps.

Meyerhold's unorthodox approach to theatre also drew on the conventions of *commedia dell'arte* and Japanese Kabuki theatre. Biomechanics, as a system, went on to become an element in Soviet actor-training techniques and was incorporated into Russian training schools such as GITIS, the Russian Institute of Theatre Arts, where aspects of his work are still taught. Meyerhold embraced the Russian Revolution, but his temperament and artistic eccentricity brought him into difficulty, and he was accused of neglecting socialist realism. He refused to submit to state-imposed constraints, defending the right to artistic experiment. He suffered from persecution, his wife was found brutally murdered and he was arrested, imprisoned and executed in 1940.

Rudolph von Laban (1879–1958)

Rudolf Laban was born in the Austro-Hungarian Empire. He was a dancer, a choreographer and a movement theoretician. One of the founders of European Modern Dance, his work was extended and carried forward by some of his most celebrated pupils and collaborators, Mary Wigman, Kurt Jooss and Sigurd Leeder. Laban raised the status of dance and movement as an art form through his highly significant, pioneering work, which developed theory and analysis applied to movement practice. During World War II, Laban settled in the UK and developed his analysis of effort of workers used in occupational movement. The analysis he undertook became the foundation of a system called modern educational dance and developed as creative dance teaching in schools and as a significant part of teacher training in the UK.

Laban's important developments in movement analysis and his notation system Labanotation, include important theoretical approaches, such as eight effort actions and the concepts of time, flow, direction and dynamics in movement. He also developed the key spatial, geometric concepts of the icosohedron and the kinesphere, relating to the movement of the body in space. Laban's work on effort actions, as adapted for actors, is widely taught in drama conservatoires and universities. His work is highly regarded as offering tools that enable the actor to make informed choices as action and in role development.

Jacques Lecoq (1921–99)

Jacques Lecoq was a theatre pedagogue who developed a body-centred, creative training out of his background in mime, mask and sport. He was influenced by *commedia dell'arte* and research into the use of masks by strolling players in the sixteenth century. He worked with Italian director Giorgio Strehler, founder of the Piccolo Teatro of Milan and with him, formed the Piccolo Theatre acting school. Lecoq later opened his own school in Paris, L'École Internationale de Théâtre Jacques Lecoq, which has become highly significant for generations of actors, mime artists, movement directors, directors and educators. Lecoq departed from the tradition of the pure, silent mime, as seen in the white-face mime artist Marcel Marceau or Jean Louis Barrault. He rejected the idea of mime as a rigidly codified sign language and saw it as a component of body-language in acting and as the most essential ingredient of genuine expressiveness and emotion – beyond words.

Lecoq's school in Paris has attracted students of theatre from all parts of the world. His focus on aspects of performance that transcend language made his teaching accessible for international students. Lecoq's approach and well-developed pedagogy using movement principles, was based on improvisation, play, Feldenkrais, acrobatics, clowning, chorus work and the use of masks. His improvisational games and tasks were, by all accounts, carefully designed, encouraging students to expand their imagination and creative practice through movement. A significant aspect of his approach to performing and theatre-making was the stress placed on the use of space, and the tension created by the proximity and distance between actors and the lines of force engendered between them. Lecoq also asked his students how they could develop their work better and their suggestion became the 'autocours'. This was a task, as a group piece, that was created weekly and performed in front of all the teachers and peers in both years of the course. In the UK, the London-based, globally recognized, Theatre de Complicité is probably the best-known exponent of Lecoq's legacy and was founded by his former students Simon McBurney, Marcello Magni, Jos Houben and Annabel Arden. Among other Lecoq alumni are directors and theatre practitioners, Ariane Mnouchkine, Dario Fo and Julie Taymor; Jane Gibson, in terms of pedagogy; and UK movement direction practitioners include amongst others, Joseph Alford, Sasha Milevic Davies, Joyce Henderson, Shona Morris, Toby Sedgewick and Ayse Tashkiran.

Leonide Massine (1896–1979)

Massine was a dancer, actor and prolific choreographer known for his vivid performances with Diaghilev's Ballets Russes and the film of *The Red Shoes* (1949). His choreography included the Modernist groundbreaking *Parade* (1917), *La Boutique Fantasque* (1919) and *Pulcinella* (1920) based on *commedia dell'arte* characters. Not widely known as a movement pioneer outside of ballet, Massine pursued a theoretical understanding of movement and anatomy, as expressive body work in creativity and composition that is applicable for actors and singers.

Massine's theories on movement were aligned with expressive potential and not concerned with an existing vocabulary as found in ballet. His analytical system regarded the body as an instrument, and

used anatomical terms for movement of the body in space. He used action terms: flexion, extension, rotation, abduction, adduction, inversion, eversion for movement paths and patterns. He applied his approaches to directions in space, three-dimensional action and the geometry of the stage space. In his artistic development with Diaghilev, he had studied detail of bodily expression, as captured in the works of Da Vinci, Michelangelo, Titian and the sculptor Rodin. His teaching introduced through his tasks, subtle and nuanced use of the torso, spine, limbs and weight transference. Massine emphasized use of the upper back and shoulders, as a vital component of expressive capabilities and described the arms with their three articulations – wrist, elbow and shoulder – and ability to extend, flex and rotate, as 'the violins of the orchestra'. His teaching also stressed mastery of rhythm and precisely timed bodily action in performance, through tasks on rhythmic phrases that demanded

Leonide Massine teaching movement theory in 1968.

clarity and precision in action, through attention to impulse and arrival points.

A simple example of Massine's characterization... is the role of the Shopkeeper's Assistant in La Boutique Fantasque *(1919). The character moves with precise rhythm, using tiny footsteps and rotates his torso and shoulder girdle rhythmically back and forth to create flapping arms like an idiotic puppet. Without attention to the anatomical detail, one might miss the torso rotation driving the action of the arms for the nervous, somewhat harried character.*

Kate Flatt in Ninette De Valois: Adventurous Traditionalist. *Richard Cave and Libby Worth (eds) (Dance Books, London, 2012)*

BODILY PRACTICES

Introduced here are a few of the globally recognized practices from well-established and some ancient movement systems. Engagement with these forms will increase bodily awareness and develop subtle, yet specific, movement skills. These practices enable flow, flexibility and release of tension, and can be instrumental in giving greater knowledge and awareness of alignment, muscle use and precision of the body in action. Knowledge gained through regular practice in any one of these forms offers important insights and a greater sense of embodiment. These movement forms feed into the approaches and practice of movement directors, as instructors and creators, crucially by nourishing the connection between the body, the senses and imagination when working with performers.

Alexander Technique

Frederick Matthias Alexander (1869–1955) developed his training system as an educational process that aims to overcome habitual limitations and patterns in movement and for the development of greater body awareness. Study of the Alexander Technique helps to release tension, soften holding patterns and induce good bodily alignment to improve posture. Regular work can serve to eliminate tension habits developed in musical instrument playing, and voice production. More than anything, this approach increases awareness of body use and helps with greater economy of movement by the muscles in action. Offered as a key element of performer training in the leading drama and music conservatoires for instrumentalists, actors and singers, it is of great value in how it can subtly retrain habitual tension patterns in movement and action.

Feldenkrais

The Feldenkrais method is named after its originator, Moshe Feldenkrais (1904–84), an engineer and physicist as well as a judo teacher. It is an educational method focusing on the working of the body, which can bring about enhanced functioning in movement. Benefits of the Feldenkrais method are described as offering greater ease in everyday activities through release from tension and muscular pain. It is acknowledged that relaxation and improved breathing create well-being, as well as enhancing performance in sport, dance, music and drama. Feldenkrais is a key movement training approach at the renowned École Internationale de Théâtre Jacques Lecoq in Paris.

T'ai Chi Ch'üan

As a martial art, it is widely recognized as an important health-giving movement form, which involves slow sequences of movement. These have allegorical significance, but as a physical practice they also have health-giving properties. T'ai chi ch'üan is a very ancient form with several styles, all of which take years to master. The main forms are *wu* and *chen*, and stem from the different Chinese martial art schools of thought and action, rooted in Taoism. Movements involve working with a lowered centre of gravity and developing coordination between action, breath and weight transference, thereby creating flexibility and flow, aimed to unblock the channels of energy and release *chi*, a life force. A sense of well-being is produced through regular performing of the twenty-minute sequence of characteristic movements. For performers it is extremely valuable for developing leg strength, breath control, sense of weight, lightness and flow in action.

Yoga

This ancient and widely practised movement form needs no introduction. In rehearsal studios around the world, actors can be found with yoga mats, preparing for both rehearsals and performance. It is essentially based on a very subtle science, and as a spiritual discipline the focus is on the connection and harmony between mind and body. The word yoga derives from ancient Sanskrit and means to join or unite. Regular yoga practice aims to develop bodily harmony, and the physical benefits are concerned with use of, and control of, breath, stretching and flexibility of the limbs, as well as increased well-being both mental and physical.

Performer Georgia Tegou.

CRAFT AND SKILLS

Movement direction is concerned with expressive bodies in action and the legibility of movement within live theatre. As we do in life, audiences can feel, sense and interpret non-verbal stories, abstract movement elements, transformations and moods that lie beyond words. Movement material becomes integrated with all the means used by the performer within stage performance. Movement of actors is drawn from intention, thought and sub-text in a character portrayal. Craft, skill and authorship of the movement director are present, along with a marked collaborative sensibility required for working in a team with other creatives. Broadly, a movement director needs to be able to do all the following:

- Communicate directly with individual performers, actors, singers and so on, to generate, coach and develop their physicality.
- Collaborate, often very closely, with a production director, on how the movement language of the performers will be developed.
- Establish through invention, relevant to the specific context, the style or tone of physicality.
- Work alongside other creative practitioners and their specialism (set design, voice work, costume, fight direction or music direction).

WORKING WITH A DIRECTOR

Reading the script or source material before the first meeting is essential, as is being able to make offers as initial thoughts on how movement might be included and contribute to the production. The meeting will ideally reveal a lot about tone, taste, style and depth required, and will spark thoughts and strategies to offer. Movement director Natasha Harrison says that she arrives at the meeting with Pinterest boards, or YouTube clips and shares further visual material following up the discussion. By this means her use of terminology, planning and creative choices are made clearer, and offer a source for deeper understanding and continued discussion.

Ideally, leave the first meeting knowing something about the director's take on the work and the questions raised regarding details on the world of the play or opera and the key characters. Other clues and information could include expectations in terms of the role of movement in the production and time needed to realize the movement work and challenges envisaged. This will determine more detail about the director's expectations on the role to be undertaken such as:

- Further research and pre-planning required.
- If creating scene changes is to be part of the brief.
- The cast and the skills of the actors.

After further meetings, the brief for the movement work will become even clearer. Meetings with the designer and other creatives will inform about further detail of the concept, regarding visuals and style. As this is an organic, changing and evolving situation, further questions will inevitably emerge as ideas evolve and develop. Here is a checklist of questions following the meeting with the director to guide pre-rehearsal research or preparations:

- When is the play set? Is it an accurate, historical time-period or updated to another era or even the present?
- What research has been done and what further is needed?
- What is the movement style or form as a basis to start with?

- How much time will be allocated to movement for the overall rehearsal period?
- How long can a warm-up last and is 'company building' part of the brief?
- What tasks for improvisation will need preparing?
- What will be invented language or draw on existing material?
- Is social dance material required and what is the music world?

UNDERSTANDING THE ACTOR'S PROCESS

The actor's body is at the centre of a matrix of creation that involves their own instinct and creative process, scene partners, audience communication, text, the dramaturgies of the production and choices made with the director.

Ayse Tashkiran, Movement Directors in
Contemporary Theatre *(Methuen, 2020)*

Movement directors offer insight and creativity that show a respectful acknowledgement of the actor's process. An actor follows the director's guidance toward the realization of the script as action. Individually, and as a company, they engage with analysis and examination of the text to find the interior world of a character. The process actors undergo enables the playing out of thoughts, intentions and actions through the voice, body and the text. Actors work intuitively with their imagination, as they draw in ideas and information, internalize emotion and thought toward constructing an inner landscape for a character that is believable and authentic.

With movement work, in the rehearsal studio, the actor, director and movement director will be concerned with developing expression as non-verbal communication. Apart from systematic script analysis, actors also work intuitively and spontaneously. The actor inhabits the staging of the play creatively, working from the inside out. In development of a character, they use imagination and emotions together with the instrument of the body.

Actors' movement workshop.

Voice, movement and action are developed in an integrated way through the actor's performance.

Actor Training

You access actors through their imaginations... that's how you get the movement work out of them... when they engage their imagination, they can do amazing things physically.

Jane Gibson in Movement Direction in Contemporary Theatre *(2020)*

Aims in actor training are to encourage an integrated approach to what is required by a role. An actor's practice involves extensive vocal and movement study that develops the habit of creativity as physical and emotional fluency with the use of the imagination. Movement is part of that along with voice, interpretation and working on intentions and actions. Impressive in conservatoire training, is the inclusion of a range of movement experiences that relate to different skills. It is possible that some may rely on one specific approach from their experience of training, such as Laban work, while others will be able to draw on a wider foundation. Some actors prefer to draw on their acquired experience in a range of roles. It is always helpful to acknowledge and respect prior experience and bodily understandings in any performer.

Movement Training in the Conservatoire

Rebecca Smith Williams, actress and theatre-maker, outlined the range of movement work she experienced in her recent RADA conservatoire training, which included:

- Pure movement – formal instruction taught in black dance-wear. It included neutral movement, bodily fitness as limbering, swinging, relaxation, balancing the space, being conscious of presence and the body moving in space. It also embraces the use of massage.
- Laban – movement taught through Laban's effort analysis, with focus on dynamics and different forces within movement and its application in scene study.
- Dance – social dances from different eras and countries, for example farandole, playford dances, waltz, minuet, pavane, galliard and la volta. Costume elements were also used such as corsets, wide skirts for the women and heeled character shoes.
- Alexander technique – individual lessons designed to encourage fundamentals of good alignment, eliminate tensions, create ease and deepen bodily awareness.
- Developing the connection between the body and how vocalization is supported through use of the breath, the pelvis and diaphragm.
- Improvisation – aims included expressing emotion through the body by accessing sense memory. She recalls being asked to imagine how it felt to look at the full moon and communicate its beauty. The action (opening the shoulders, looking up) comes from allowing the emotion to come through from the physical memory.

HOW DO PEOPLE BECOME MOVEMENT DIRECTORS?

Experience versus Training Methods

There are a range of pathways to follow for those wishing to become a movement director.

Many specialists in movement work arrive at working in this professional role through diverse branches of training and varied career paths, with valuable experience as performers. They may have worked with text-based theatre, physical theatre, acrobatics, dance or martial arts. Some people shift roles from choreographer to movement director. There are diverse fields of movement direction and ways to diversify and specialize. A picture emerges of a movement director as someone who draws on, and develops, their craft from a range of resources within themselves. Essential tools and skills of movement directors are covered fully in the following chapters, but a summary here indicates that they:

- Acquire knowledge about the body through multiple, dance and movement experiences.
- Develop strategies for creating in the moment, as a live experience.
- Synthesize information and translate material drawn from research into ideas.
- Direct, coach and support performers in the studio.
- Collaborate with directors and others throughout the theatre-making process.

Movement Direction – Building on Experiences

Many movement directors diversify from a career as an actor or as a physical theatre performer and can capitalize on their professional experience and prior training. They will be familiar with the actor's process and are at a distinct advantage in understanding the creative delivery of character, intention and embodied emotion. In training they will have engaged with the work of key movement pioneers and have benefited from a lineage of tradition in actor training. It is important that movement directors build on this experiential knowledge and technical understanding about what is happening within a body in motion. Key also is learning to navigate successfully within a collaborative arena, working with a script, text or a libretto.

Skills in Practice

A movement director primarily needs movement knowledge and skills, but observation skills and being in the moment during rehearsals to perceive change, action and clarity are essential aspects of the role. Critical engagement takes the form of 'reading' the unfolding action and recognizing elements or moments that could be developed or changed to deepen or clarify the emergent story or character. Work with the performers might mean analysing how the movement or action occurs, and what part of the body, dynamics or weight transference in the action could work more effectively. The analysis and creative feedback to the performer is an exchange that involves well-developed verbal skills. All dialogues and exchanges need listening skills to navigate working with the director, performers and the rest of the creative team.

CAREER PATHWAYS

The route or pathway into becoming a movement director is different for everyone and there is no single identified route. Here, in the words of these practitioners, are examples of the different routes they have taken to develop, find their place and work successfully as movement directors in live theatre production. Career development can involve finding opportunities for studio observation whenever possible or seeking work as an assistant to an established movement director. Post-graduate provision is to be found in the MA MFA Movement: Directing and Teaching at Royal Central School of Speech and Drama (*see* Appendix I).

Anna Morrissey

My early theatre-making experiences were facilitated by an enlightened arts programme at my London comprehensive school. Apart from dance and drama at GCSE, there were theatre-making opportunities for productions realized within the school. It was a time of building confidence and discovery, along with collaborating, taking decisions, making choices about movement (before I knew what a movement director was), as well as working on choreography and incorporating lighting for the staging of it.

I took a degree in anthropology at Cambridge, studying human behaviour, including the understanding of tribes. This has proven to be incredibly useful in my approach to the world of a play but also in seeing the playing company as being like a tribe. After Cambridge, rather than entering a conservatoire, I followed my own programme of training in London, whilst supporting myself. It included a range of dance forms, techniques and courses, including those at Birkbeck and Morley College. I then entered the first cohort of the now well-established MA MFA Movement: Directing and Teaching at RCSSD, which showed me the path to where I am now.

Jonathan Goddard

I have always been interested in choreography, and as a dancer with Rambert, I would spend my lunch breaks experimenting with making work and creating material. As part of a fund-raising effort for Rambert's new building, I was offered an opportunity, with another Rambert dancer (Gemma Nixon), to create something for a Human Rights Watch charity gala at the Royal Court. The piece involved choreographing to some spoken text by Martin Crimp. I met resident director Simon Godwin who was overseeing the evening and we started discussing the development of the choreography. Through this experience I realized how much I enjoyed working with a director, which was a totally new experience. I could see he was thinking in a totally different way from dance practitioners and yet he also enjoyed working with dance. After this experience I continued the relationship by asking him to look at some of my choreography, and over a period of about two years, he would come and watch, and we would talk about what he saw in my work – we got the opportunity to share in a creative exchange.

After I left Rambert in 2012, I began to diversify my practice as a choreographer, and started tutoring at the Architectural Association, exploring the role of movement with students of interdisciplinary work. I also had the opportunity to participate in workshops and rehearsals for the West End production of Charlie and the Chocolate Factory *(2013) with choreographer Peter Darling and associate Ellen Kane. It marked my first time working on movement with actors rather than dancers and I spent time teaching and passing on the movement I had helped develop for the grandparents in the show. Later in the same year, Simon Godwin asked me to join him as a movement director on a production of* Strange Interlude *by Eugene O'Neill at the National Theatre (2013). This was my first experience of working on a play; it was a great learning curve and a hugely different world to the bubble of being in a dance company – one I really enjoyed. I began a journey into the world of theatre movement and the creative challenges the work offers.*

Diane Alison Mitchell

I never trained in dance but spent my childhood doing everything physical. I was in every dancing competition at school, as well as doing all sports, such as hockey, athletics and rounders. I also trained for a time as a hurdler. Within my Caribbean community, I was a member of a steel band during my teenage years, performing throughout the West Midlands at festivals, carnivals and sporting events.

I left the UK and moved to France and started going to dance classes religiously – I 'found' myself in those classes. I followed teachers giving training in the dance practices of Benin, Guinea, and Congo. And before I knew it, I was often at the front of the class – they put me there for others to follow. I went on to perform with the dance companies of various teachers. It was serious, committed fun but I had not yet envisaged it could be a career.

When I returned to England to attend university in Brighton, I joined Mashango Dance Company and began making formal steps into dance. I went on to work primarily with companies such as Adzido, Sakoba and Movement Angol, whose work was deeply rooted in African and Caribbean techniques – a way of how the feet connect to the floor, a yielding and insistence to gravity, contrasting undulations and pulsation of the spine, isolation of body parts in percussive interplay, the creative collaboration with the drummers and percussionists, the use of breath, sound and voice within the movement.

I had my eye on the MA MFA Movement: Directing and Teaching at RCSSD for about two or three years, but it took time for me to realize I could apply even though I was not an actor. Once there, I knew this would be my new path. I had always been drawn to narrative and storytelling – a place where dance and movement exists and so much more.

This became the window that I looked through – seeing movement in life, in stories via a deep understanding of what is close to me in my heritages – physical, cultural, social and educational.

Diane Alison Mitchell in rehearsal with Tiata Fahodzi.

CHAPTER 2

THE PROFESSIONAL CONTEXT

Creativity is not simply a matter of letting go. Serious creative achievement relies on knowledge, control of materials and command of ideas.

Sir Ken Robinson in All Our Futures, NACCE *Report (1999)*

ECOLOGY OF EXPERTISE

Context

Within contemporary theatre production, several factors need to be considered regarding the context and environment in which the movement director exercises their creativity. In the collaborative world of professional production, all the creative practitioners experience ever-changing issues that arise in terms of possibilities and constraints. There is a sense among professionals that the end goal of the performance is more important than yourself, your own needs or desires. All involved, in each department, work with craft, skill and imagination, toward quality of delivery using collaborative, inter-personal skills and a confident understanding of their own place in the scheme of the production. Within this ecology of expertise, the ground rules require a state of preparedness to exercise creative imagination, including being able to 'read the room' and the emergent activity.

The Creative Team

A creative team is comprised of a group of talented experts involved in the imaginative realization of a live theatre production. The director and producer from the venue or theatre company choose the creatives involved:

- Director.
- Designer.
- Lighting designer.
- Movement director and/or choreographer.
- Voice or dialect coach.
- Assistant or associate director.

Depending on the scale of the production, other practitioners could include:

- Sound designer.
- Video projection designer.
- Fight director.
- Magic or illusion specialist.
- Aerial choreography specialist.

PRODUCTION SUPPORT

Production Management

The support provided by the production manager and technical coordinator is instrumental to realizing the process and result of the creative vision.

- The production manager is on board early in the process, to oversee the logistics involved in realizing the ideas of the creative team, and the impact of the set design concept on the overall budget.
- The technical manager is ultimately responsible for the technical delivery of the show, such as the

OPPOSITE: *Ballroom of Joys and Sorrows* at Watford Palace Theatre 2012. Performers: Jack Jones, Tim van Eyken, Lizie Saunderson, Amir Giles and Marie Chabert.

materials, actual nuts and bolts of the set build, the lighting rig, sound effects and video projection.

- The wardrobe supervisor oversees all elements of costume, footwear and wigs, and manages the costume budget.

Stage Management Team

During rehearsals, the stage management team creates a link between the entire creative team, the technical department and the work in the rehearsal room of the director, movement director and fight director. Daily rehearsal notes are compiled by stage management and questions that arise from the staging and any impact on the props, design and visuals that may occur. Stage management also documents the staging and action, creating a 'book' of the show for all the cues. They distribute a schedule for the rehearsal room sessions, and any further studio sessions that may be required for movement work with individual performers. Any questions affecting a movement director's work in relation to that of other departments can be addressed first to stage management and then to other departments.

Production Meetings

During the rehearsal period, there are scheduled weekly production meetings for all creatives, stage management and the departments involved in the visual elements, so that everyone is up to speed on the technical details. Advance schedules are discussed and planned in detail to maximize the smooth running of the technical stage rehearsals. This means that, in the process of creation, there is a truly collaborative spirit, with attention to each person's detailed needs, and respect for the many involved in working creatively toward an outcome that is a shared creation. Movement directors are advised to attend production meetings, particularly when aspects of their work involve interaction with other departments.

Backstage Support

The stage management team is essential backstage in performance, along with a body of technicians who manage scene changes, move the set, operate flying or hydraulic pieces of the set, and care for the props and so on. The lighting and sound technicians are seated at operating desks with headsets on and able to receive cues from the deputy stage manager for changes and effects.

- Company stage manager oversees all aspects of the cast needs – for example, accommodation if touring, wellness, rehearsal etiquette, and monitoring onstage and offstage activity.
- Deputy stage manager has a prompt desk backstage and 'calls' the show, meaning all the cues for changes in lighting and sound, calling technical crew for scene changes, such as flying set pieces. The DSM calls the actors on the half hour, quarter hour and five-minute calls to the stage. They also stop the show if there is a problem.
- Assistant stage managers fulfil a range of roles, but one person may be assigned to props.
- Wardrobe departments manage costume maintenance and provide staff for dressing and quick changes.

Health and Safety

The movement director is expected to be conscious of the aspects of health and safety pertaining to movement work with performers. This will involve provision of warm-up and preparation, levels of fitness and managing anything that may be considered a risk in the movement work. The stage, the surrounding wings and rehearsal room safety are the responsibility of stage management, but it is worth outlining what the work will entail and the relevance of footwear or use of bare feet. For any contact with the floor required (rolling, lying down and so on), ensure that the floor is clean and swept, and remind performers to wear suitable clothing.

Physical warm-ups are deemed essential, and artists should attend these or be given time to do their own. Knowledge of existing injury and health in performers is required, including the level of fitness and suitability for the work. It is advisable to fully check if professional performers who are wheelchair users or challenged by other long-term

Jenny Ogilvie with singer James Newby rehearsing a movement sequence for *Greek* (Scottish Opera, 2017).

disability issues, visible or invisible, are cast in the production. In community or participation work, levels of fitness need to be ascertained at an early stage with appropriate warm-ups and material devised for the participating group. Safe-guarding issues will also be significant when working with minors and vulnerable adults (*see* Appendix I).

Contracts

Movement directors as creative artists work freelance and are mainly engaged on a short-term contract, for a specific project by a company. As an independent or a freelance practitioner, the movement director is considered responsible for their own National Insurance contributions and tax payments. It is advisable to take out public liability or professional indemnity insurance before starting work. It is also worth establishing that you are working only within your own professional skill set. If a movement director is asked to supervise anything that involves a specialist skill for the performers or that of other practitioners (such as acrobatics, aerial or bungee wires, or fight material), the work should be declined and the venue should hire the appropriate person. If you do not have an agent, the billing for the movement director in the contract should be established and its position in the hierarchy of credits. It is also worth finding out to whom your programme biography should go and by when.

REHEARSAL PROCESS

Preparation

In addition to creative planning, the movement director needs to prepare mentally for any new production. There will be a new company of people with whom to share the challenges and demands presented by the script and concept. Interpersonal skills will be needed, as are aspects of self-knowledge, confidence and a grounded awareness required to lead on the movement work. It is important to develop a capacity to 'read the room', to know who is present and how to operate in the scheme of what is taking place. The rehearsal room is the space in which the movement director will lead their

work and which they will 'hold' at times, in the place of the director. It is also a place in which to take a back seat, share the journey by observing the work of the director and performers.

On Day One

Before the warm-up on day one, check out the size of the studio and that your voice is audible, especially if there is a large group. Learn the names of the performers and attend the 'meet and greet' session for the whole company and staff from the theatre venue, often held on day one. Introduce yourself to the stage management team and assistant director, who you may not have met but will be working with for the entire rehearsal process. Recognition and appreciation of the assistant or associate director's role is an important factor as they will be working closely with the director. Information about your movement strategies and developmental decisions will need to be shared regarding the schedule and rehearsal process.

Studio Rehearsals

The number of weeks of studio rehearsal for a production can vary. On a new play or play being devised, the rehearsal process will be longer and last possibly eight weeks in the studio. The process may include a period of R&D (research and development) to try out or test aspects of the script. A normal studio rehearsal process is around four to five weeks before technical stage rehearsals. Pantomime production rehearsals last a maximum of two to three weeks, but musical theatre or opera rehearsal periods can be much longer. With an opera or musical, the first few days are given over to music learning and individual coaching before the staging begins. Separate dance or movement calls are held for the devising of musical numbers or sequences of movement. On a play there may be a read through of the play on the first day, followed by analysis and table work on the text and individual character detail. The movement director is often asked to provide a full company warm-up each day – following or preceding a vocal warm-up. Individual movement calls with actors or smaller groups on specific scenes requiring movement attention will be scheduled as rehearsals progress.

The Schedule

Whatever plan the director and movement director may have made in advance, the schedule will follow a rhythm demanded by the play and following the director's approach. Generally, the schedule for each day is announced by the afternoon tea break on the day before. In opera, the schedule is planned further in advance and can be considerably less flexible. Costume fittings, calls for fight direction, dialect and vocal work must be taken into consideration. Regular run-throughs of work of scenes or for each act that have been established will be scheduled for specific times.

Costume, Footwear, Props

It is customary to have a rail of rehearsal clothes, particularly for work that requires period costume, shoes, corsets and so on. If specialist garments are worn, and particularly if they affect movement, it is worth making sure that there is either the real thing or an equivalent available in rehearsal. Corsets are important as they affect the carriage of the body and as they are restrictive, prevent a lot of movement, and affect the use of weight and ability to bend. If possible, find out from the designer what the footwear will be and ask for it to be made available for the performers as soon as possible. Often rehearsal shoes will be made available from the outset, as significant health and safety issues can exist with the relationship between floor surface and footwear. Performance shoes will have non-slip soles and heel height is a further consideration. If props are used, or furniture such as specific chairs or tables, ladders or beds, it is important that they are available so that any work with movement can be rendered viable and safe.

THE COMPANY 'WARM-UP'

The movement director will be expected to offer a suitable warm-up devised for the needs of the production. The 'warm-up' is a cover-all phrase for the bodily preparation of performers for a rehearsal

and throughout a rehearsal period of a particular work. Making clear what the needs of the movement work are, in terms of preparing the body, is a vital discussion with the director on planning and realistic scheduling with regard to content. It is important to cover not only the basics of what's needed, but to ensure that the actors are equipped with tools to take responsibility for the movement work they will carry forward.

Planning a Warm-Up

Each project will present different needs and require the movement director to make a carefully considered approach to physical preparation for the ensemble of performers. This will require a range of approaches in terms of instruction, guidance and creative facilitation. Movement material can focus on energy and muscle use, breath, skeletal awareness, stamina building, as well as instilling a presence, being in the moment and in touch with the body, connected and grounded. Planning and preparation will depend on the individual approach, but it reaps rewards to guide performers through material that relates to the script and can be drawn on in the evolving creative work.

Check-In

With any new group, first, it is important to address safety in the performing company and find out if anyone has injury or existing 'damage' in the body. A check-in with performers is advisable and finding out if any of the material being developed or offered might cause a problem for them. Opening a dialogue area on this in relation to individual bodies is of value and alleviates problems almost before they arise. In general, the movement director needs to offer ways of releasing tension and opening awareness in the body, so that performers are in a receptive state with a neutral body for entering the work.

Warm-Down

At the end of rehearsal, before performers go home, it is helpful to add warm-down exercises. These are extremely useful if the material in the play causes emotional tension, such as in plays with psychological or physical demands. Depending on the context and nature of the work, the encouragement of a sense of well-being, both physical and mental, will be supportive toward any individual struggles with the material and its impact on the body.

Finding an Individual Approach

Every movement director develops their own unique approach to the warm-up and designs it as fit for purpose in rehearsals and how the actors enter the world of the play. The use of metaphors helps performers to embody ideas and concepts, and imagery and terminology can be developed relevant to the play as a shared, common source and resource. It is helpful to address focus and interiority from the outset. Working in a circle with the material, rather than commanding from the front of the room, means that the work is led and guided as non-hierarchical action. It is worth recognizing how an individual movement director uses language that adds value and nourishes ideas and performers during the process.

Establishing Focus

Performers can be asked to close their eyes and imagine looking into a black velvet curtain. This allows the muscles at the back of the eyes to soften and encourages interiority, whilst remaining aware of the rest of the group and listening to the room. Added to this, is a focus on the breath and paying attention to breathing patterns. Further, it can be a moment to sense that the surface of the skin can soften, the knees, hips and soles of the feet can relax, allowing the body to be receptive and open. The use of imagery in a warm-up stimulates the imagination and awakens the senses, all helping to achieve focus and interiority.

It is useful in a short, standing warm-up to include the following:

- Lengthening the spine – imagine an air space between each vertebra.
- Sense the top of the head floating upwards way from the base of the spine.

- Breathe quietly into the lower abdomen and focus on in and out breath.
- Expand awareness of peripheral vision and sense of the space around oneself and others.
- Allowing the weight to drop down through the hips, into the legs, softening the knees.
- Feel the soles of the feet in warm sand and wriggle the toes.
- Sense being in a warm shower with water flowing down your back and then front.
- Reaching out to the edges of the *kinesphere*.

Warming up the joints, muscles and ligaments can be simple tasks that everyone of differing physical abilities can achieve to mobilize the body. A range of short, slow and steady sequences for the legs, lower back, activating the major joint combinations in the body will warm and oil the muscles and tendons. Include a sense of 'moving through warm oil' for shoulder rolls, spine rotations, hip rolls, head and neck actions, side bends, full roll downs and recovery taken slowly, all mobilize the spine and muscle groups. Knee bends, with an Achilles' tendon stretch place emphasis on grounding and sensing the legs connecting to the pelvis and centre of the body. It is helpful to offer balance exercises and also introduce a sense of expansion and release, enabling the performer to make a connection between the movement and the surrounding space. Ankles, wrists, hands and elbow joints need to be sensed as ready for action though rotation, flexion and extension.

Offer questions to performers to help increase bodily awareness:

- Where is your weight when you are standing or sitting?
- How balanced and poised is the head on your spine?
- What tension can you sense and where? Can you soften the area and release it?
- Can you sense the space you are in and the breadth of it?
- How connected to the ground do you feel?

- What situation have you brought into the rehearsal room with you that you can feel in your body and that you don't need here?

CREATING AN ENSEMBLE

The warm-up session in the first few rehearsals can facilitate the development of the ensemble as a creative and communicative entity. A cohesive group is needed to work creatively, productively and safely, with shared commitment to the process that enables a play to come alive. This process can offer a sense of agency and trust; increase the creative flow in the room through group instruction and improvisation on different themes. These strategies will help to remove inhibitions, enable receptivity and connection, which are all essential to create a company spirit. It is important to include the whole group, as well as working with pairs and small groups on problem-solving tasks.

Games and Dances

There are many well-tried theatre games, name games and ball games from different practitioners and traditions that engage with play, awareness of risk versus safety and avoidance of needless competition. They awaken the senses and focus and, as designed by children, they are universal,

A group warm-up exercise.

A spiral dance.

with straightforward rules for fairness (for exam-ple, all forms of grandmother's footsteps, catch, it or tag, sticky toffee and so on). Games and group dances alone will not prepare the body adequately for deeper work, but as group tasks they provide ice-breaking, connection and loosening up of hier-archies within new ensembles.

If appropriate, a simple folk dance could be included wherein the company move in the same walking rhythm linked as a chain, in a spiral pattern. The winding in and out of the spiral allows the whole group to pass one another and connect by seeing and feeling present with everyone else.

Into Rehearsal

A physical warm-up can move easily on to creating movement material for the staging as it becomes established. The movement director can lead on the development of shared movement language and technical learning, as well as the development of material through tasks drawn from research. Improvisation frameworks can be prepared from ideas drawn from the script, the research using

previously discussed themes that can be drawn out. These ideas possibly exist only in movement, beyond words, as embodiment of ideas, thoughts and feeling. This process can reveal much about meaning, relationships and character.

> *...for me, working with movement to release aspects of the play is crucial at the early stages of the process and gives an informative organic result, developed through the bodies of the actors.*
>
> *Femi Elufowoju Jr, director, speaking in a master class on the Doorway Project (2021)*

Enabling Creativity

Creativity involves intuition and imagination. It is important that an ensemble or company of perform-ers feel that their generosity, in terms of creative offers of movement material, are acknowledged and valued. Finding moments to appreciate everyone's efforts, including the movement director's own, especially if the material doesn't end up in the final staging, is worth its weight in gold. Performers with experience

WARM-UP TO DEVELOP A GROUP SKILL

The voice coach had just done a vocal warm-up and I was asked to follow on with a physical warm-up. The director had asked me to work out quick and easy ways to teach some basic slap-stick, to help identify who could be drawn from the ensemble and appear throughout the play as a small comedy troupe. I recalled from my training at Lecoq, and working with Johnny Hutch, specifically, work that involved throwing and manipulating chairs.

I started with the actors just throwing one chair around the circle. This was followed by asking them to throw and catch more precisely using a 'fixed point' with the chair. Then we worked in pairs with someone holding on to a chair and the other person having to fight for it. This way we began a process of working toward the realization of a basic slapstick routine. One actor complained to stage management of an ache in his side, and I was asked for health and safety reasons not to continue with this. I recall from my training encounters with Johnny Hutch as being very much from the 'no pain, no gain' school and it was not possible to evade tough issues with him – you just need to keep going come what may. Unless we are given more time to practise, and if there is caution on the part of the actor and stage management, it can be hard to make progress with the development of a challenging idea.

Joyce Henderson, Movement Director, in conversation (2021)

realize that this is all part of the process, but less experienced people need reassurance. Elements of movement creation, training and skill development across the rehearsal period offer the following:

- Ways to awaken the physical imagination.
- Develop physicality suitable for the action of specific parts of the play.
- Activity to build the company spirit as a community.
- Ways to create a sense of play and a common energy.
- Introduce action suitable for sequences without text.
- Develop action for a scene change.
- Create the physicality of a specific contemporary style or one from history.

SCENE CHANGES
Movement for Scene Changes

The creating of movement for scene changes is an important aspect of the movement director's practice. Their work with the ensemble on moving scenic items to change a setting, place or context, can avoid black-clad technicians arriving to clear furniture and objects. It is important to establish which scenic elements or furniture need handling, the weight or bulk and, practically speaking, whether wheels may have to be attached to heavier items. The stage management will be crucial to the process of delineating the space, providing a floor mark-up in relation to the set design, with further marks or a 'spike' for the placing of objects handled by the performers. It is probable that scene-change

SCENE CHANGES IN PRODUCTION

The Provoked Wife (1697) by John Vanbrugh at the RSC (2019)
Tashkiran talks of how discovering the 'seed' of a scene change can reveal the movement language for the whole production. For her work on *The Provoked Wife* by John Vanbrugh at the RSC (2019), director Philip Breen suggested that every scene change could be punctuated by music and musicians. This led to a decision that the whole ensemble would activate every scene change. This opened a rich, choreographic potential that revealed the society of the world of the play. In this production, there was one scene change that was the most complicated onstage and offstage moment that she had ever movement directed.

Harry Potter and the Cursed Child (2016), directed by John Tiffany, Palace Theatre London (2016)
Steven Hoggett reports that the London production of *Harry Potter and the Cursed Child* (2016) has seventy-five scene changes. As there are no black-outs between scenes, each scene change is designed to use movement and action in different ways. Hoggett raises the question to be solved, which concerns what action can be drawn on for the scene change? He can then make a connection with the preceding scene, by using movement and action from it during the scene change action. Alternatively, elements can be introduced in the scene change and, for continuity, used in the scene that follows. Scene-change action involved organizing material with the performers that kept the story flowing throughout all the action. He suggests also that transitions between scenes can appear to embellish, magnify or even explode a moment in the action of the story. He describes one scene change that required the movement of a flock of chairs, transforming into a schoolroom, and during its creation, he asked the performers to imagine that the desks were pulling them around the room. For a quick change in *Harry Potter and the Cursed Child*, one of the Dementor costume changes was timed to exactly one minute forty seconds, so a movement event was created to last for that exact time, so that the story kept moving forward seamlessly.

rehearsals will be given time as the staging of the play comes together, rather than left to the end for technical rehearsals.

Expressive Potential

Ayse Tashkiran, in July 2021, shared her views on scene change work. She suggests that there is expressive potential in scene changes and in how they give leeway for play and devising of movement within a narrative drive that engages the ensemble of actors. They can become signature events of a production, as in Theatre de Complicité scene changes, for example. In their transformations, everything flies – desks, books, chairs, or pieces of paper are manipulated by the company and then suddenly, at the end of the transition, there is a new image that takes us forward in the narrative.

Tashkiran also observes that scene changes often need to happen fast, but sometimes they can be used as a 'breath out' and a way to offer an audience a moment of pause or contemplation. They can become magical and complex. It's likely that the audience does not watch for meaning, so much as 'live' the experience of the change as action. So, the energy and dynamics become important for the movement director. In practical terms, there needs to be careful choreography to organize action, people and objects moving at speed. Fast-moving traffic and the safety of handling weighty, awkward objects are always at the forefront of the movement director's considerations. This can necessitate lots of planning with the design and the stage management teams. In tech, scene changes can become a rich collaboration of movement with other creative input, such as lighting and video.

A SHOW GETS BORN

Technical Rehearsals or 'Tech'

Following the weeks of studio rehearsal there is the crucial stage in any production when the studio work transfers to the stage to be made ready for the audience. Technical stage rehearsals follow on from a final, studio run-through, attended by the entire creative and technical team. Technical rehearsals are a period of intense work in the theatre and can sometimes be a gruelling and demanding time. It is also a moment of discovery when the show or production will get born, when all the work of the creative team comes together, staging, action, movement and sound are integrated with the visual elements, making a linked entity from humans and hardware. Technical rehearsals are not normally where new ideas are initiated, but there may need to be many adjustments to the work created in the studio. It is a demanding time for the performers, with so much to think about beyond their portrayal of a role. Sometimes producers attend, hovering around, some nervously, others with observations, while the creative team are working. Their notes and concerns may not be so helpful at this stage, but once there is an audience their view will be very valuable.

Performer Jordan Ajadi rehearsing on stage at Watford Palace Theatre.

CHANGES MADE DURING TECHNICAL REHEARSALS

Les Misérables, directed by Trevor Nunn and John Caird, RSC at the Barbican (1985)

The staging had been devised in the studio without the monumental and iconic moving structures, known as the 'barricades' from John Napier's iconic, original set design. The scene where the beggars of Paris first emerged, singing 'Look down, look down' had been staged from an idea using the movement of the ensemble. They began in a huddle, on the ground, like a bundle of rags centre stage, moving from detailed exploration as an improvisation, and gradually emerging as people who inhabited the space during the first part of the number.

In the technical rehearsal this movement-inspired action just didn't 'read' powerfully enough. After a speedy discussion, the scene was restaged by placing the actors upon the different levels of the epic, barricade towers, as they moved slowly toward the centre of the stage. The actors emerged gradually, in character from the skeletal architecture of the set, as if from within the stairwells and balconies of a poverty-stricken Parisian tenement.

Is it Working?

In technical rehearsals, the pressure of production with all the elements and the results of the studio work come to fruition. It can happen that scenes or staging (which felt and looked great in the studio) may not read successfully in the context of the scene once on the stage, in the set. There are many reasons why this can happen, and further work is needed, for example, in terms of placing the material better, changing aspects of the staging or adjusting the lighting or sound. This can affect everyone's work and needs considerable calm and negotiation. Collaboration involves empathy and consideration by the entire creative team to make a scene work successfully. As a movement director, it is important to feed in your observations, to continue working with the performers but bear in mind how much new information or detailed thought you are asking of them, when there is so much else going on.

I had an enlightening experience moving the play from the studio on to the stage. On one occasion, something was not working right during technical rehearsals in a section that the movement director had arranged. It had worked in the studio but not in the set, and the lighting designer pointed out the problems created for the lighting of the scene. There was no time to restage the action, which involved a couple moving quite fast and engaged in kissing and embracing at different points around the set. I discovered that a very helpful note given to the actors by the movement director, Shona Morris, solved the problem entirely. From this I noted a big difference between the pressure of needing to restage complex activity in a scene and seeing how one clear note offered could solve a problem. The note clarified how everything could work – for the actors, the lighting designer and in the entire scene.

Brigid Larmour, Director, in conversation
(spring 2021)

PREVIEW PERFORMANCES

The Audience

A production begins to take life when the work is exposed to the audience in preview performances. The audience and their reactions over several performances, inform the director and creative team of anything that might need clarifying or re-shaping. This is particularly true of specific scenes, which may be in the wrong order, and a shift, cut or repositioning will clarify the narrative. Rehearsals continue with full technical support on each day of previews. For the director of the show, it will become clear what needs to be cut, shortened or developed if there are dips in attention or overuse of an idea. After every preview performance, technical notes are given each night by the director for the full creative team, production and technical staff and the stage management team. Performers' notes are given the next day before further rehearsals and technical adjustments. The navigating of this, by the communication and sharing of views between director and movement director, is vital before giving notes to the performers and offering feedback in a way that avoids coming between the director and the actor. Sometimes a shift in lighting or sound state, rather than cutting material, can help, or a series of precise acting or movement notes can solve a problem. These changes need to be processed and any adjustments need to be 're-teched' to help the performers and operators to get used to the changes.

LES MISÉRABLES, BARBICAN THEATRE (1985)

As with the development of any new musical or play, the preview performances provided an opportunity for scene or lyric re-writes, with cuts or additions. Some scenes were reworked or staged in a different order, which meant that the details of each change affected the work of all creatives, so the performers and creative team had to have further technical adjustments.

Each morning, at 11.00, before rehearsals, the company assembled in the auditorium for notes from the night before. New lyrics and cuts were distributed and discussed. After lunch rehearsals continued, so that all changes were rehearsed technically, and incorporated in the preview performance that night. This went on for the ten days of previews until press night.

Pre-Performance Warm-Up

Once a production is in performance, a pre-performance warm-up may be required. This is usually held for the entire company before the half-hour call, giving time after for that almost sacred and uninterrupted period of time, needed by the actors or singers to focus and prepare for the stage. The design of the warm-up is shared between director and movement director, and it helps greatly if this is practised by the performers during the preview performances. The aim may be to develop connections between specific actors, the entire group or for individual movement needs developed within the play. A good pre-performance warm-up should offer a segue from the daily life of the performers into the world of the play. Many performers have their own personal rituals as pre-performance preparation and it is worth respecting those and what individuals need to do. In some cases, a skill needs to be maintained so that it doesn't slip or so that the continuity and precision of the work or stamina required need attention and care.

PRESS OR OPENING NIGHT

This is a time of celebration and the culmination of all the work undertaken in rehearsals, tech and preview. There are many thanks to offer to all the departments who have contributed to this moment of presentation to what may become a long run. It is also a moment of heightened nerves for performers, as not only will an audience of industry professionals attend, but relatives, friends, the critics and reviewers too. First night gifts and cards are exchanged, and an after-show drinks gathering is usually held, so there are plenty of distractions that make focus harder to achieve. Some directors quietly give their notes and encourage the company to treat the occasion as 'just another show' in which all the work so far continues. It is not advisable at this moment to introduce new elements to a warm-up, give complicated notes on the material or offer criticism that may be unhelpful or cause worry. More than anything, offering calm, supportive words of appreciation to the performers and an assurance about following their journey, will lift spirts and support the necessary control of performance nerves, and finding focus despite the distractions.

PERFORMANCE MAINTENANCE ON A LONG RUN

Movement Director Jenny Ogilvie – *A Midsummer Night's Dream* (1596), Director Joe Hill-Gibbins, Young Vic (2017)

For this production of *A Midsummer Night's Dream*, Joe Hill-Gibbins and designer Johannes Schütz created a space with three elements in the raked, amphitheatre-style auditorium at the Young Vic. This created an oppressive ceiling suspended over the performers and audience, with a back wall that was one giant mirror and a pit of ankle-deep mud that covered the whole playing space.

The mud pit made the terrain physically tiring for the actors, so that the exhaustion the characters feel as they become more and more confused was really tangible. They also emerged from their night in the woods much less clean than when they went in! As the movement director, as well as creating the physical language for the show, I had to ensure that the actors did regular strength training to build ankle-knee-hip stability for this rough terrain.

Movement Director Kate Flatt – *A Dream Play* (1901) by Auguste Strindberg, Director Katie Mitchell, National Theatre (2004)

A Dream Play was in repertoire with several days off between a run of performances and had precise movement material sequences throughout the play. A specific warm-up was devised and written out for the actors. A dance captain from the cast was appointed to lead this, to be done pre-performance. It included ballet sequences and waltzing, which were both incorporated into the action and needed constant care and maintenance, so a moment was added to refresh sequences from the actual staged material. This was discussed with the actors and a request made that they should do the warm-up material also on their days off. With the backing of the director, the idea was strengthened, so that

the beautiful work the actors were doing would not slip or deteriorate over time. The actors were very responsible and did what was required. On a re-visit, to give notes to the actors, it was discovered that a tough set of core strength exercises should be added. This was because back problems and strains emerged through moving furniture and racing in high heels to cross to the other side of the stage for quick changes, using an unusually long route around the back of the theatre auditorium. The physical problems only came to light after the previews and the exercises were added to avoid injury. Safety in terms of keeping an eye on issues arising from the play is an increasingly an important job in terms of show maintenance.

Discussion during a technical rehearsal.

CHAPTER 3

THE EXPRESSIVE BODY

The human body is an amazing masterpiece. With the senses we see, hear, taste, smell and touch the world, drawing its mystery inside us. With the mind, we probe the eternal structures of things. With the face we present ourselves to the world and recognize each other. But it is the heart that makes us human.

John O'Donohue, Benedictus
(Bantam Press, 2007)

THE PERFORMER'S BODY

This chapter offers ideas in terms of movement direction approaches and looks at a performer's body as an expressive instrument. Every movement director needs to develop their own personal toolkit for their approach, which can be adapted and applied in a range of creative contexts. The toolkit will reflect their embodied movement knowledge, in terms of background, experience, training, aesthetics, personality and ways of seeing action through their own lens. Movement directors draw from a range of backgrounds, theories and practices, which may reflect the work of the Key Pioneers referred to in Chapter 1. The movement director will also rise to the challenges offered by a script, score or libretto and the world it presents for the actors or other performers.

Working with the performer and the expressive body will involve:

- Understanding of anatomy, muscle use and coordination.

OPPOSITE: **Sam Curtis and Joy Constantinides in** *Soul Play* **(2010).**

- Appreciation of differing skill levels and abilities.
- Conscious awareness of what makes action expressive.
- Rhythmic, dynamic and spatial considerations.
- Character development as physical behaviour and body language.
- Thought, emotion and feeling legible through physicality.
- Energy, breath, weight and flow in movement.

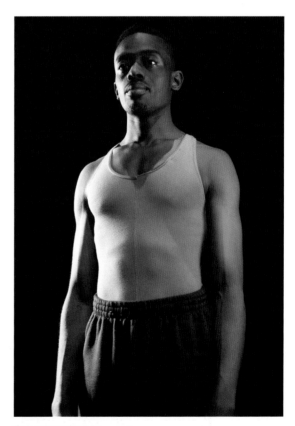

The neutral body.

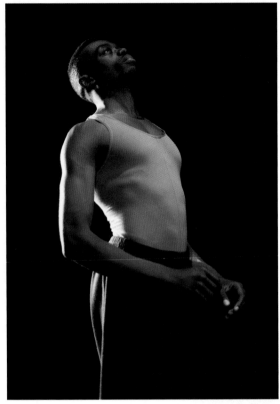

- Imagery and metaphors to aid physical performance.

Infinite Variety

Ideally, the body of the actor or other performer is in a state of neutrality, able to offer expression through the body as an instrument. The receptivity of the neutral body is one aspect that actor training aims to achieve, and it offers a palette for creation of types of action and development of characteristics. An important awareness is about what is felt, along with any held patterns or habitual muscular tensions. The infinite variety of human bodies offers a wide range of movement possibilities, as well as limitations. Movement directors both observe and respect differences between bodies. Their work will support performers by clarifying what is happening in the use of the body. The performer playing this bodily

Use of the spine and upper back.

instrument can achieve a conscious embodiment of a characteristic and what it expresses as perceived by the audience. States of mind and feeling can be observed and sensed through subtle shifts affecting the musculature (whether consciously or unconsciously). The movement director needs to be able to not only read these, but be able to help the performer to be aware of them and the detail they offer.

ALIGNMENT AND UPRIGHT STANCE
The Expressive Spine and Torso

The use and action of the spine is a fundamental part of creating expression. We don't need to look further than footage of meerkats on wildlife programmes to realize the importance of the signal given by the spine. Groups of meerkats show alertness with their lengthened spines as they perch

Rotation and use of pelvis.

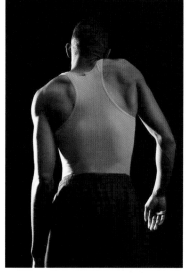
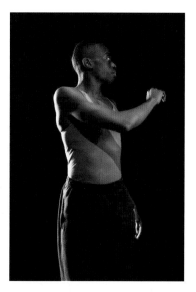

Use of shoulders.

upright to assess danger. We find it amusing to witness, but one main tool for the movement director is to realize how an alert extension of the spine can give out a message to be read by the audience. Attached to the spine are the head, shoulder girdle, ribcage and pelvis. Other varied, subtle shifts of skeletal elements (for example, the spine in relation to the vertical) can give a richness to reveal differences between people, and by simple means become part of how a physical or behavioural characteristic can be created and observed.

A Question of Gravity

Humans, and all living beings – trees, plant life and animals – strive against the force of gravity to be upright as they grow. Emergent life makes adaptations and develops differences through growth, and according to circumstances and conditions for life and survival. In humans, this can manifest in body shape and conjures up thoughts of how trees grow old, gnarled and twisted, yet stoically upright defying gravity, with the ability to withstand and move with the wind.

TASK: CREATE A CHARACTER BODY USING A SKELETAL SHAPE

Ask performers to take a neutral stance and be aware of the alignment of each of the sections of the torso, which can be divided as follows:

- Upper back and use of sternum, including detail of shoulders, neck and head.
- The torso from the waist.
- The pelvic girdle.

Make a shift off the vertical using or emphasizing the sections of the body to build a surprising but subtle shift away from the upright and balanced vertical axis. The three parts create a sense of a three-note musical chord – or discord. Create a bodily structure initially, which can be animated by a walk. An exaggerated construct will emerge.

- Allow rotation of the shoulders, a lift or drop of the sternum, slight inclination of the upper chest, movement to the side forward or back and use of the upper back.
- A bend forward from the waist, a slight incline backwards of 5 degrees from vertical, a rotation.
- Thrust the pelvis forward or backward or tilt upward to one side.
- Add a raised shoulder or a lowered or inclined head.

Character development:

- To give a sense of normality, and to downplay the exaggeration, think of the character doing an everyday task, such as going out to buy a pint of milk. Sense how that idea can make a character simpler, less demonstrated and more believable.
- Animate the emerging physicality that could suggest characteristics through the vertical, upright use of the spine, empowering a sense of survival, as a purpose to keep going.
- Observe how the choices can be very small shifts from the neutral stance but still read.
- Give this physical character a short history. What does the stance suggest? Ask a partner to give a name to the character.

Upper back and arms.

Picture an elderly man, a priest, crossing a square in Paris. In his black garb and a beret, he leans forward, bent at the pelvis, with his torso at an off-axis angle to his legs. His head is leading. He walks slowly but purposefully about his business, leaning on his walking stick but with a determinedly upright energy. Conversely, picture the stance of a man on a hot spring day, in a Mediterranean country, with his lengthened spine, sternum and upper back lifted in joyful acknowledgement of the sun. This is in stark contrast to the image of the downward-dropped sternum and upper back, lowered head and gaze of someone walking purposefully, challenged by rain on an overcast, wet and windy day in the UK.

By observing human beings around us from the point of view of their stance, we may see a spine that is slightly twisted, a torso inclined off the vertical axis, a tilted pelvis, shoulders hunched and different levels of tension in the musculature. The sense of verticality and the need to defy gravity and strive upwards, and its many shades of difference, seem to encapsulate purpose in life.

MOVEMENT – LIVING MATERIAL

The Impulse to Move

Any movement begins from an impulse with a point of initiation within the body – an instinctive reaction without a thought, resulting in action. An example of this is to imagine your frail and elderly aunt about to tumble over. You move, without thought, to reach out with an immediate impulse to stop the accident from occurring. A very different movement would occur if the impulse for movement is to touch the arm of someone who is distressed and needs consoling. Movement unconsciously reflects thoughts, feelings and mood of everyday life. The task for the movement director and performer in realistic theatre production is to make the movement reflect the psychology in a way that is believable.

Movement Elements

Rudolf Von Laban offered an analysis of movement with four broad elements: direction, speed, flow and weight. This breakdown, using four simple broad categories, can be used or applied in a creative context.

Direction

This encompasses spatial orientation, direction of travel within a space and connection to the surrounding space. It also suggests purpose, a sense of design and shape and expressive qualities of the body using different directions of the stage space.

Speed

This encompasses time, along with duration, tempo, rhythm and the perceived feeling that the experience of time can generate through movement. Compare the speed of two people in deep conversation, walking on a beach with that of two small children and a dog playing with a ball. Never mind the activity, the speed alone communicates a feeling.

Flow

This suggests liquidity and a sense of constant motion, as well as the dynamic range of effort and energy to be found in movement. Think about the quality of flow in movement and the contrast between smooth, free-flowing motion versus spasmodic, withheld, sustained (or as Laban calls it 'bound') flow.

Weight

In movement, this suggests gravity and resistance to it. It also encompasses transference of weight

TASK TO EXPLORE MOBILITY

This simple exercise explores aspects of mobility and offers a way to examine different movement properties. There are dozens of words associated with mobility – we all skip, walk, leap, bound and run, but these expressive terms capture qualities of action: amble, crawl, slither, shuffle, skitter, grovel, scuttle, lunge, lope, swing, lurch, bound, spin, leap, shift and glide.

Choose a movement action from one of the words above (or provide your own). Create about 30–40 seconds of material that encapsulates what the word indicates. Develop the fragment of movement to have a beginning and ending.

Focus on one of these four elements:

Speed – fast, very fast, walking pace, snail's pace, slow motion.
Direction – advance, retreat, rise, sink, follow, evade.
Flow – momentum, force, effort, energy, sustained, contained.
Weight – heavy, limp, wiry, strong, weak, slumped, light, airy.

- Explore a clearly identifiable quality in the chosen action, such as a fall at a slow speed or a series of fast lunges, airy spins or leaps. Examine the quality of the motion and how it occurs in the body.
- Add further detail and focus on a different property, for example weight. Observe what needs to change for the movement to become richer or more detailed.
- Continue down the list by giving focus also to direction and then to flow in the movement.
- Now, alter one of the properties radically, such as speed or direction.
- Imagine a character performing the material and provide a reason or context for the action.

TASKS: WALKING AND CREATING DIFFERENCE

How Do We Walk in Real Life?

Working with a partner, observe in detail how the other person walks.

- Without verbal analysis, imitate the gait and walk of the other person with as much precision as possible.
- What do you notice about placing of weight, and width and length of the step?
- Watch the carriage of the upper back, position of the pelvis, the degree of tension or ease in the way that they walk.
- Learn the walk with precision, then demonstrate what you have learned.
- Share observations about the difference or similarity between your walks.

1000 Ways of Walking

It can be useful with a large company of performers to explore the mechanical action and the contrasting ways of walking or running to find multiple differences.

As a task, do the following exploration, with the performers' choices and sense of bodily action as central. Ask them to:

- Experiment with placing the descending or lifted weight in different ways through the foot, the ball of the foot, the centre or the heel.
- Choose the width between the feet – wider than the hips, narrower than the hips or tracking a single line like a tightrope walker.
- Decide how 'turned out' the legs and feet are, for example like a ballet dancer or confident athlete, or turned in like a reluctant child.
- Choose a pace length – a stride can be longer than is comfortable or as short as half the length of your foot.
- Examine the speed – fast or slow – or normal walking speed?
- Try raising the heels a centimetre and walk without the heels touching the floor. What happens?
- Experiment with a sense of lightness or heaviness, or even try to walk without disturbing the air.
- Explore how a shift of weight reads in action.
- 'Animate' the walk to reflect a mood, intention or topographical change.

Explore three different ways of the above, number them and perform them, keeping the specifics and accuracy of each one clear and precise in use of the anatomy.

Choose one of the 'walks' and imagine doing it simply going to buy a pint of milk – so that the nuance of it become less demonstrated and more an everyday action.

Observations:

- What do you observe in the body and in the work of others and its effect?
- Watch the differences that emerge between the people in the room and the choices they make.
- What do you notice when it became more 'everyday' and less heightened?

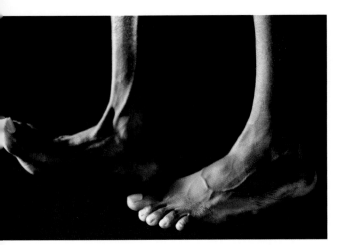

Awareness of feet.

THE WALK AND CHARACTER DIFFERENCE

Think about ways of walking. What is happening as the weight falls? Walking can be experienced as catching falling weight. It is also propulsion – experienced as a drive through the pelvis with impetus from the lower back, resulting in the weight moving and being caught by the foot on landing. The expressive use and transference of weight can indicate much about intention, a state of mind, health, demeanour and inherent purpose of the figure walking. The act of walking or running as a change of weight can have immense variation, whether from person to person, or the circumstances. The effect of the walk on stage will tell the audience a lot about what is going on. In the use of entrances and exits, if someone is in a hurry, we observe a change of speed, possibly tension in the use of the body with the head leading and shoulders raised. This might indicate a serious situation and its effect on the person arriving on stage.

involved in the motor skills of walking, running, swaying, retreating, advancing and so on. The term also broadly encompasses the concept of how weight is carried in the body and with that the expressive quality that can be used to denote mood, emotion or thought.

Walking.

Walking task.

CREATING DIFFERENT CHARACTERS THROUGH A WALK

Ask yourself the following and provide answers through devising action:

- How would a ghost or other supernatural figure walk?
- What is the difference in the way of walking or running between a five-year-old, an eleven-year-old and a fifteen-year-old?
- What shows seniority or old age in a walk?
- What is significant about a pregnant woman walking?
- How does a dancer walk?
- How does a tired person walk?
- How does a labourer or someone bearing heavy weights walk?

BREATH

Patterns in Breathing

Katie Mitchell suggests that an audience reads emotion through a change of breath pattern in the actor. To expand awareness of using breath expressively, here are examples of different types of breath patterns. As you actively work through them, observe the rhythmic pattern that emerges for each:

- Sighing: short in-breath and long out-breath.
- A gasp of surprise: short in-breath, hold and release.
- Panting: short, quick, repeated breaths.
- A peaceful baby when asleep: continuous, light, steady and gentle.
- Laughter or crying: spasmodic, repeated, a bit uncontrolled and chaotic.
- Yawning: long and deep in-breath with an equal out-breath.
- Sneezing: short and sharp.

TASK: CONNECTING BREATH TO MOVEMENT

Explore the use and application of focus on breath in abstract movement or in a realistic context of a scene. Aim to reproduce the shape of the breath in movement as you follow the pattern or shape of the breath in time. With a pattern involving repetition, such as panting from running, choose how long it will last. Explore material and action as three to four contrasting breath patterns from the list above. Share your results with others and observe the differences you find.

Create two to three short, naturalistic movement fragments with a performer, which follow the shape and length of the breath pattern, observing the sense of movement within them.

- Locate an impulse in the body at the beginning of the breath pattern, then follow the movement through to a stillness.
- Explore the action as realism, with intention or in a situation that will create differing dynamics. Work to make the underlying intention clear through the breath change.
- Add the movement to a situation in which the change of breath indicates difference of emotional reaction.

Observe:

- What happens in the pattern of in and out breaths?
- Is the breath high in the chest? Or lower in the abdomen?
- What other sensations can you observe in the body?
- Discuss ways that these breath patterns can be applied to intentions or circumstances within a given or imagined scene.

Unconscious gesture.

GESTURE

Gesture is a field of movement work that has many books all to itself. Gestures are codes in movement that are a crystallization of meaning, generally using the arms, head and upper body, and are essentially a non-weightbearing action. There are different categories of gesture that can be commonly understood as non-verbal communication. Gesture can be used to create style and characterization, as fragments or detail of movement that can be descriptive or demonstrative, and both conscious and unconscious.

Types of Gesture

It is worth observing, when around Mediterranean peoples, how gesture is initiated, and how the upper back and shoulders move before the hands or head, or words are uttered. When I worked in Japan, I experienced formal polite gestures as social codes and body language, which were important to interpret. Just as a foreign spoken language cannot be easily understood, so body language can be perplexing, with a requirement to respond appropriately and with risk of creating a social gaffe. In business, there is training in the use of body language, not only for people to present themselves better, but to provide formal, non-emotional delivery that does not communicate thought, intent or purpose in striking a deal.

A very important gesture language is British Sign Language (BSL), which, as an official minority language, enables audio-impaired people to converse and make spoken text understandable for them in live performance situations.

Gesture in opera is traditionally heightened and stylized. A connection to thought or sub-text is made with gesture in relation to a sung phrase, with attention to timing and dynamics of the music phrase, which is very different from that of an actor in a play. In contemporary opera productions, use

Business body language.

Gestures: menace, dejection and foppery.

of gesture is continually being developed to make performance of opera relevant for our times.

Rhetorical Gesture

This term refers to formal expressive gesture used to illustrate speech and clarify meaning in the art of oratory and public speaking. This practice relates back to classical Greek and Roman times, developed in Renaissance theatre and continuing into more recent theatre practice in the nineteenth century. The actor Henry Siddons produced a book of *Practical Illustrations of Rhetorical Gesture and Action* (1822) and the few engravings from it are included here to depict emotions and thought as gesture and demeanour. The book includes accompanying observations that indicate Siddons' interest in the task of codifying gesture language and its meanings as a form.

Naturalistic Gesture

Actors become artful at incorporating naturalistic gestures in a nuanced and expressive way that

Clasped hands.

allows us to forget that they are born from choices made in a rehearsal room, through examination of thoughts and intentions. This is the opposite of more abstract, heightened gesture, which can be used for demonstrative, comedic or stylistic effect. There is the notion of finding 'where' in

Popular hand gestures.

the body the impulse is felt to initiate a gesture. Gesture can be delivered from 'my heart to you' but where does that gesture land and how? The development of conscious use of rhythm in relation to breath, thought and emotion in gesture is essential.

Popular Gesture

Gesture can be playful, poetic, sometimes abusive and can indicate a wide emotional range of pleasure, excitement, disgust, annoyance or even sexual innuendo. As a silent language, it can be universally understood, or it can be secret and known only to a few – as it once was used by the criminal underworld in the city of Naples. Gestures are also culturally specific and examples include the high five, a V sign, touching fists, shrugging, blowing a kiss, thumbing the nose and the heart depicted in the shape of two hands.

Gesture in Dance Genres

In nineteenth-century ballet, mime sequences included a distinct codified language of gestures developed to an extent from the theatre practice of Italian *commedia dell'arte*. Mime gestures used in traditional ballets explain sections of the story and are a handed-down tradition. In South Asian dance forms, codified gestures known as *mudra* are intricately woven into dance as storytelling. Gestures in vernacular usage can be found incorporated into popular street dance forms such as break dance or hip-hop and as clearly recognizable

gestures they are used in sequences for accents and emphasis.

Ritual Gesture

Gesture in symbolic actions, such as prayer poses, the sign of the cross, genuflecting (kneeling) or touching palms, are part of rituals. These are again codified actions and may show reverence or respect and differ greatly according to culture and religious heritage. They can be ritualized, as in kneeling to pray, curtseying, bowing, army salutes, the handshake and so on.

Ritualized gesture.

TASK: THE 'QUESTION AND ANSWER' GAME IN PAIRS TO EXPLORE A DIALOGUE THROUGH GESTURE

Ask performers to stand or sit in a circle, paired together.

- Performer A makes a gesture to Performer B that embodies a question.
- Performer B makes a gesture in response that embodies an 'answer', then poses their own question to Performer A.
- Continue this procedure in pairs or expand it as a 'round' passing the questions on around a circle.

Pay attention to:

- Scale and size of gesture.
- Timing and rhythm.
- Detail of hand, head and initiation point in the torso.
- The end point and making the gesture 'land' on another person and resonate.
- Transfer of weight.

What do you notice?

- Are both the question and answer legible, precise and clear?
- Can the performers and spectators read the action?

BODY LANGUAGE AND PHYSICAL PORTRAITS

Authenticity is what the actor offers, and its translation is read by the audience. If the basis of the instruction and movement design is over-contrived, it doesn't work.

Steven Hoggett, Movement Director, in
conversation (2020)

How is the body perceived and how is it inhabited? The movement director's skill lies in identifying and creating with the performer the type of body for a character or ensemble. Many types of physicality can emerge from exploration by the actor, guided by the movement director. More on this can be found in case studies by practitioners in this book

but some ideas for practical exploration could include:

- The child's body.
- The ageing body.
- The desiring body.
- The punk body.
- The ravaged body.
- The angry body.

Les Misérables, Directed by John Caird and Trevor Nunn, RSC (1985)

In the scene set in the red-light district of Montfermeil, during the upbeat musical number *Lovely Ladies*, is the moment when, in Fantine's story, she is revealed as a prostitute. She is driven to the desperate situation to support her daughter

TASK: CHARACTER PORTRAITS FROM TEXT AS WAYS TO DEVELOP MATERIAL THAT HAS VALUE AND FEEDS THE IMAGINATION OF THE ACTOR

Victor Hugo's character descriptions in his novel *Les Misérables* are vivid and cinematic in how they capture the movement behaviour and physicality of many different individual characters. These few provide a poetic source for the creation of the characters as movement portraits.

Use the spine work, breath, flow and weight elements referred to in this chapter to explore the gait, carriage of the spine, breathing patterns and gestural characteristics to create a physical portrait that brings one of these characters to life. The movement sequence need only be brief, but seek to capture the movement as a portrait, as if in a thirty-second film clip. Share the results and observe what reads well.

- Madame Albertine
  She is described as a lady who was 'not more than thirty, dark-haired and handsome, was wont to gaze remotely about with big, dark eyes. Did she in fact see anything? She seems like a ghost and to glide rather than walk... it was doubtful if she even breathed... To touch her hand was like touching snow. She had a strange spectral grace and a chill enveloped her wherever she went.' (p.439)
- Babet
  The picture of this gang member is of someone 'lean and cunning, transparent seeming, unfathomable. One could see daylight between his bones but nothing in his eyes. A man of affectations, a fluent talker who underlined his smiles, and put gestures in inverted commas.' (p.623)
- Montparnasse
  He is described as 'urchin turned vagabond, a vagabond turned desperado, smooth, effeminate, graceful, strongly built, pliant, and ferocious...'. Further, his dandy qualities are described as 'a fashion plate living in squalor'. He was a murderer, with a 'slender waist, a woman's hips, chest and shoulders of a Prussian officer, cravat meticulously tied, a flower in his buttonhole, a blackjack in his pocket'. (p.624)

From *Les Misérables* (1862) by Victor Hugo, trans. Norman Denny (Penguin Classics, 1982)

Cosette. With the women of the ensemble, there was a rehearsal where we discussed what the life of prostitutes in 1832 might have been like and how their bodies might have looked and felt. Disease and consumption were rife, and the women as sex workers not only needed to survive and feed a family, but may also have had a drug or alcohol habit, such as taking laudanum, an opiate and a poison from the belladonna plant, which was once used to widen the eyes. Using work on the spine, pelvis and positioning of the weight, the results of their investigation and choices, created body images that were very much less than lovely and had an almost ghostly fragility. The actors' bodies took on both a distorted and asymmetric stance, as with rehearsal skirts provided, they then offered themselves to attract and invite customers, with an alluring pose, as if on display. In the staging of the scene, to the upbeat song lyrics, the women surrounded their pimp and sold themselves energetically to the harbour district clients. Moments between verses, when the women were off duty, they used their weight differently, slumped, exhausted and defeated by the situation. The effect created was closer to grotesque images from *Los Caprichos* (1797–98) of Francisco Goya, rather than a raucous or playful concept for these 'ladies of the night'.

Character portrait. Fashionable impudence.

CHAPTER 4

MOVEMENT IN SPACE AND TIME

I can take any empty space and call it a bare stage. A man walks across this empty space, whilst someone else is watching him, and this is all that is needed for an act of theatre to be engaged...

Peter Brook, theatre director, in The Empty Space
(Penguin Classics, 1st edn, 1968)

PERFORMING SPACE

The iconic Epidaurus arena in Greece has an impact even as we only imagine the performances that took place there in earlier times – in full sunlight. Alternatively, the feeling of an auditorium as a dark, enclosed space can be one of a vivid, shared experience. Watching a street performer do something extraordinary, very close to us, amidst the ordinary pedestrian bustle of daily life, offers yet another way to experience theatre.

What is Being Experienced? Scientific Research and Audiences

An intriguing scientific discovery about audience behaviour when watching live theatre, shows its importance and, seemingly, why we enjoy the experience of live action.

Research in 2017 has found that watching a live theatre performance can synchronize your heartbeat with other people in the audience, regardless of whether you know them or not. The heart rates of twelve audience members were monitored at a live performance of the West End musical *Dreamgirls* (1981). Alongside individual emotional responses, the audience members' hearts responded in unison to what they were watching, and their pulses were observed to be speeding up and slowing down at the same rate.

Experiencing the live theatre performance was extraordinary enough to overcome group differences and produce a common physiological experience in the audience members.

Dr Devlin, Researcher, UCL
Division of Psychological and Language
Sciences (PaLS), Encore Theatre (2017)

Imagined Space

In Shakespeare's time, as in Ancient Greek theatre, no elaborate decor was provided and audiences of the time imagined the Forest of Arden or Dunsinane, King Lear's heath and the violent storm at the opening of *The Tempest* or *Othello*. In our technological age, with moving scenery, digital projection and advanced lighting equipment, one might forget that theatre-making is fundamentally a means to awaken the imagination. A movement director's sensitivity to the space and the narratives that occur within it in relation to the geometry and architecture, are key to the creation of the feeling of life within the space. The performers' embodied imagination and their connection to the stage space, all enable the audience's enhanced perception of the action on the open stage. It can be transformed to create mood and atmosphere. This is as significant for single performers, as for ensembles.

OPPOSITE: **Skyscape.**

SPACE, TIME, FEELING AND ATMOSPHERE

Task 1 Visualization of a Specific Place and its Associations

- Ask your performers to shut their eyes and focus on their breathing. Take a minute or two for this.
- Imagine or recall a specific place, which could be from early childhood or a place you visited in a dream. It may have strong associations from the time you spent in it. What is it like? Imagine yourself inside that place.

Here are a few examples, with different temperatures and atmospheres, even without human beings:

- A nursery where small children have been playing.
- A place of worship, church or temple that is empty.
- A railway station, very late at night, in winter.
- A bar on a warm Friday night – a group were chatting but have just left.

Observations:

- How open, closed, dark or light is it? What is above your head and under your feet?
- What is its humidity or temperature like?
- What sort of rhythm is present even without the occupants of the space?
- What pulse speed can you sense? Establish what the pulse speed is and what other rhythms are present.

Task 2 Creating Small Group Activity in an Imagined Place

- Close your eyes and imagine looking into a specific interior space or room. Imagine looking through glass or a camera lens and that you cannot hear any sounds of activity there.
- Create 30–45 seconds of material with a small group, in silence, which takes on the rhythm of the place.

- Focus less on the action of the people who were there before, but more on the 'after image' of how the space feels with the memory of the rhythm of movement in the imagined space.

Observations:

- Stand back from what you have made and look at it objectively.
- Use sound, text, or music to enhance the material in the task.

Task 3 Creating Spatial Tension

The descriptions listed below can suggest a series of imagined atmospheres. Choose one and work with the ensemble on movement material alone to establish the tension or atmosphere indicated.

- Dangerous: predatory, hectic, edgy.
- Serene: peaceful, quiet, still.
- Expansive: wide-open, broad, released.
- Confined: imprisoned, limited, trapped.
- Exposed: revealed, vulnerable, solitary.
- Airy: light, bubbly, breezy, free.
- Secretive: private, hidden, defensive.
- Intimate: close, sensitive, and interpersonal.
- Ritual: formal, focused, structured.

Observations:

- How can you use proximity between people, body contact or negative space?
- How can the feeling in the space be affected by the space?
- What music or sound do you imagine could accompany the action made?

Creating Atmosphere

Movement and action inhabit and colour the space to create the feeling that occurs in time. In the studio, it is important to imagine how the stage space will appear, with entrances and exits into the space, as well as shaping the atmosphere created by the action within it. Key to this is being able to sense the 'rhythm of the space' as atmosphere and feeling in the space through the action. The tasks here are designed to awaken the performer's imagination and sensitivity to the aspect of the whole stage space, which, along with the movement director's work, can affect the perception, feeling and imagination of the audience.

Creating the Atmosphere of a Space and the Feeling of Rhythm

The next task is designed to awaken the imagination and increase sensitivity as to how we can create rhythm of action to achieve feeling and atmosphere through movement. Working from these images of landscape or places, the aim is to capture the atmosphere of enclosure, open sky and so on, by finding a pulse, speed and rhythm within three-dimensional action with performers in the studio space, and eventually a stage space. Working with a small group, explore proximity, body use and enhanced embodied imagination with a feeling of time.

Sunrise.

Tower.

Forest path.

TASK: FEELING THE RHYTHM OF THE SPACE

- Use one of the images given in this section and ask the performers to look closely at it for one minute. Ask a performer or ensemble to imagine themselves within the space.
- After a further minute, ask them to assess what the 'feeling of the rhythm' is in that place.
- Use the atmosphere and transform the feeling of it into action, as movement in the space.
- What is the effect on the body, breath and sense of relaxation or tension?
- What type of action occurs with a group?
- What underlying pulse do you sense in this place? What rhythmic pattern is felt with that?
- Arrive at 45–60 seconds of material for five to six people that responds to the space.
- Create action that captures the feeling of time in the image, in three dimensions.
- Transform the atmosphere of the studio by capturing the 'feeling of time and space' drawn from the image.
- What music or text do you imagine could accompany the action you have made?

Car park.

MOVEMENT AND THE FEELING OF TIME

The movement director can be a guide for the actor in how to articulate intentions and thoughts clearly in time, by considering the rhythm, duration and speed of any specific action or gesture. There are many possible ways for movement to shift away from realism toward a more abstract set of actions. Heightened moments can highlight the sub-text or delineate shifts in mood in a non-realistic way, because of a focus on how time and rhythm are used. The movement director's skills can create moments of slower or faster action to intensify feeling and sharpen the mood, and to highlight moments in the action of a scene.

Time and Intention

It is well documented that any motion or action on stage can be driven by underlying emotions, tensions, thoughts and behaviour in the characters that are not directly scripted or spoken. In this area, both the director and movement director work with the actors' interpretation and their process on timing of action, breath and gesture. Movement directors need a well-developed understanding of how to sensitively support actors during rehearsals with the director's work on underlying emotions, tensions, thoughts and behaviour in the development of action.

Time Perceived

A conscious relationship with time factors and their effect on the movement can shift the perception of mood, feeling or psychological state of a character – as if painting with hues and shades in portraiture or writing a melody, or punctuating a poem. The challenge in movement direction is to develop a super-sensitivity to the timing of motion and how that is not divorced from a sensitivity to the context. This implies everything in the space, location and setting, furniture and props on the stage.

Key Aspects

The key terms inherent in the broad category of time when applied to movement:

- Tempo – speed of action, can be measured as beats per minute (bpm).
- Duration – how long does something last or what time is taken up?
- Rhythm – a proportional pattern of motion and stillness – with accents and pauses.
- Pace – the feeling of time passing in the playing of a scene and as the play is watched.

Silence, Pause or Stillness

These are important visible time factors, which punctuate and give shape to action, as found in the phrasing of music, through editing or within the shots of a film. Stillness can provide an important area of dramaturgy, by articulating small segments or 'beats' of material related to narrative, encounter and any dialogue that may have silences or unspoken sections.

Sarah Fahie, movement director, describes how her work in both opera and plays involves 'sealing the moment', as in shaping an actor or singer's movement in relation to intention or thoughts, so that the audience's eye and attention is drawn to a significant moment. This enables the audience to catch up with the unfolding narrative – whether that be through word or the movement action in the play or opera.

Scripted Pauses and Silences

The timing of movement and action in a play is a consideration throughout in relation to movement work. Debbie Tucker Green's plays, for example, have detailed markings in the script to denote the pauses and deliberate interruptions she wishes for in the text delivery. It gives the movement director an idea of how silences or text overlaps occur, which gives clues to, and can inform a lot about, rhythm and tempo of action.

THE EYE AND SENSING TIME

Time encompasses speed, duration, pace and, significantly, the rhythm of action. It is without doubt for the movement director a significant and nuanced factor in all that happens on stage and the way that the play is experienced by an audience.

The only sense that is fast enough to keep pace with the astounding increase of speed in the technological world is sight. But the world of the eye is causing us to live increasingly in a perpetual present, flattened by speed and simultaneity.

J. Pallasmaa, The Eyes of the Skin *(2013)*

Juhani Pallasmaa writes eloquently on perception. Here he is speaking about how new technology in our age affects the way we see. We are accustomed to moving images in advertising and bombarded by the speed of editing, with images and sounds flashing persuasively into our brains. In our age, the dominance of digitally created images and the potential disturbance or effect on the brain, caused by photons from mobile phone or tablet screens, is an area of scientific study. Our digital world undoubtedly affects what we see in live, human action and Pallasmaa seems to suggest that we might be losing sensitivity to other experiences of time. Live theatre involves the interplay of action in time and space. In a production of Anton Chekhov's *Uncle Vanya* in the West End (2020) with actor Toby Jones, directed by Ian Rickson, there was a palpable, clearly felt sense that time was slowing down in the last ten minutes of the play. It offered the watcher a sense of stillness, allowing the text and its meaning to resonate more deeply. This skilful use of pacing, used so subtly, served to deepen our experience of the play.

CINEMATIC TIME IN LIVE THEATRE

It is inevitable, in our increasingly visual world, that techniques from cinema have infiltrated the world of theatre-making and are visible in abstract passages of movement as heightened storytelling in sequences, or for scene change action. Approaches to editing and shaping time found in cinema offer an intriguing way to play with the medium for live theatre, creating abstraction and heightened moments. Altered time is addressed in the next section and offers tasks to be explored with performers to develop sequences. One of the most often used aspects is that of slow motion but there are other examples, such as ripple-dissolve, freeze-frame, jump cut, rewind or fast-forward and a recent innovation (used in *The Matrix*) of bullet time, used by movement director, Steven Hoggett, in his work. This work also develops the observational skills of the movement director and the notion of movement seen through the 'window of time', as Anne Bogart refers to in her book *What's the Story* (2014).

Influences on Theatre Movement

> *The dominant, all-powerful factor of the film image is* rhythm, *expressing the course of time within the frame.*
>
> *Andrei Tarkovsky, film director in*
> Sculpting in Time *(1987)*

As in art house cinema, we can perceive that this is also true of theatre. The considered use of movement in stage action, its pacing and speed, can give the sense of time passing, and an experience of time within the world of the play. Andrey Tarkovsky, the great poet of cinema, in his series of masterful films *Mirror* (1975), *Nostalgia* (1983), *Stalker* (1979) and *Sacrifice* (1986), introduces unfolding images of motion in real and altered time. Tarkovsky's vision, along with his technical and artistic responses to the art of time in cinema, has influenced the work of British theatre director Katie Mitchell and her approach to directing. Her productions have utilized time factors meaningfully, through the technology of foley interventions and live video feed on stage, especially in her production of *The Waves* (2006), a devised play based on Virginia Woolf's novel.

TIME DEVICES

When used in live action, the following approaches can be used to treat movement as if it was a piece of film. They offer dislocation, as a choreographic and abstract intervention, heightening and drawing attention to the action and taking it away from 'normal' realistic behaviour.

Slow Motion

As we watch slow motion, what is it that becomes heightened? This is undeniably a powerful way to heighten feeling and expression on stage. It can be panic, fear, joy, hope or falling to one's death. The speed change is clearly noticeable, and the performers provide a visual tension in the stage space. In addition, it can bring a moment of emotional intensity or a sense of anticipation, as an almost dream-like event is drawn out and lengthened within a work.

Les Misérables (1985), Directed by Trevor Nunn and John Caird RSC (1985)

The slow-motion moments in this production were very specific in their use and created heightened emotion with the movement and music, in a series of sequences that contributed to powerful storytelling.

TASK: WORKING WITH SLOW MOTION FOR A GROUP

Before starting this improvisation with the performers: awaken the peripheral vision, awareness of breath and of the others in the group. Do a series of slow, deep, knee bends, on two legs and one leg to awaken conscious use of a lowered centre of gravity and balance.

- **Tag.** Ask a group of 12–14 people to play 'tag or catch'. Be precise about the rules and purpose of the game. Then ask the group to use the same material of the game, but now in slow motion. At the clap of a hand, or at the sound of a whistle, all shift gear to slow motion. Examine what the gear change means and what happens in the body. How does the physicality of 'not wanting to get caught' become more expressive at slow speed?
- **Snowball fight.** Ask two groups, at opposite ends of the studio, to improvise a snowball fight, with all the different emotions and dynamics involved. Explore the fun of playing with the material of snow: making snowballs, aiming and seeing a reaction, keeping some eye contact, being hit, ducking and so on. Examine the action for the movement paths in space, effort and flow in the playful atmosphere. Then switch to slow motion, keeping the speed as uniform possible.
- **Street Riot.** With approximately 7–10 performers in each group, placed at opposite ends of the studio, improvise a street riot.

    Group A – angry youths rioting, with the action of throwing – imagining pebbles or cobblestones.
    Group B – police defence – imagining the need to stoically hold the line and also to avoid injury.

    As the improvisation plays out, Group A pays attention to throwing – as in what happens in the body, the force, embodied emotion in the action, focus of aiming and so on. Conversely, Group B pays attention to the detail of reaction, avoidance, ducking, standing firm amidst the attack. Encourage vocalization. Now in slow motion, watch and observe the heightened emotion, keeping the action clear and precise.

Technical body use:

- To help individual balance, begin slow-motion sequences by dropping the weight, lowering the centre of gravity and controlling the breath.
- Awaken a sense of sustained speed with breathing coordination.
- Groups in slow-motion sequences need a cue to begin and end that is understood by all.
- The intensity and purpose of the game, the force and the energy used to throw, reach out or touch, may mean that the movement can momentarily revert to normal speed and lose the sustained flow needed.
- Ideally, no 'counting' takes place (it can help to establish simultaneous action, but in an exterior way).
- Clarify the relationship of the new, slowed down action to any music used.

Observations:

- What is experienced in the body? What must happen to accurately reproduce the action once slowed down?
- Can the speed be maintained? Does it get more difficult if the action continues for longer?
- Is the action clear? Are the story and emotion still present at the slow speed?
- How does the speed change give a different quality to the action?

Panic and Confusion

In Act I, a group of Parisian city workers are seen escaping from a runaway cart, which the lyrics explain is careering out of control along the narrow street behind them. They run fast around the stage, gathering others along with them in a peloton-like pack. Their body language tells us, as they occasionally glance back, that they are afraid. Arriving upstage left (USL), they then shift, using a music cue with an abrupt pause and immediate speed change to slow motion. On a diagonal path, the close group seem to jostle, showing the chaos of a stampede. A girl is lifted high out of danger, a man falls forward and rolls over, some glance backward, open mouthed at the unseen danger, some make a silent scream of fear as they try to escape. The action is at uniform slow speed, as if the heart rate and breathing had also slowed down. Then abruptly, on another musical cue, normal speed resumes and we see the actual cart, crashed centre stage with a man trapped beneath it. Throughout this sequence, there is a tension created by the short, but eloquent, shift in speed.

Celebration

Act I Finale starts as a group of students gather around their revolutionary leader Enjolras, in a Paris square. They have recruited citizens of Paris and enter the stage, greeting each other excitedly, then stop and sing out to the audience, 'The time is now, the day is here!'. They then break into a moment lasting about twenty seconds, of group slow-motion, with action that affirms their collective feelings of hope, excitement and joy. They and the audience believe that they are on the brink of the undeniable and certain change that will come from the insurrection.

Death

Act II, at the end of the battle on the barricades, the students, while fighting to the last, are all shot by the army. They die in slow motion with their action individually timed across the phrasing of the powerful score. The moment of expiry and last breath heightened this way, is a tragic, poetic, unfolding moment. Each actor had to focus on the shot, the impulse, impact in the body and the fall to negotiate a journey for their body within the complexity of the barricade

ANTIPODES (2017) BY ANNIE BAKER, CO-DIRECTED BY CHLOE LAMFORD AND ANNIE BAKER, NATIONAL THEATRE (2019)

Sasha Milevic Davies describes her movement work for the production:

Part of the brief from the two directors concerned moments between the scenes and time passing. The action took place with the actors seated around a table, telling their stories. There was nothing else on stage, as part of the design, which could show that time has passed, except the body. I needed to create a sense of time not just passing but jumping between the scenes. I worked with all the actors on movement to make time appear to jump – like for a jump-cut edit.

For each scene, we [myself and the actors] had to work with bodily action throughout, around the large conference-type table of the design. This meant that when a character talked or told a story, then they also moved, and the others listened attentively. It was totally about using a rule for the physical language and gesture. Each of the moves was very consciously shaped for each of the characters being played. It appeared to begin with naturalism. As a group, the actors played with moments of specific, structured, simultaneous action (yet not in identical unison), then they returned to a continuation of their stories.

structure. It was important to keep a believable reality, within the heightened collective expression, as each individually timed trajectory was completed, simultaneously, at a uniform speed. A dramatic and epic stage picture was created and then the revolving stage took the image away from the audience's view.

Creating Slow Motion

To achieve slow motion and to find uniformity with its use, it is important to decide on, and analyse, precisely what action or scenario is taking place. The Task games offer that and help to develop group awareness and dynamics. The tasks are not about creating rigid unison but simultaneous action, with each individual performer conscious of their action and its quality in real time. With group tasks, it is important to establish the material of the game, but now in slow motion. Agree with the group on the pulse speed for

Heightened emotion at the RCSSD.

TASK ON BULLET TIME

Ask two people to move across the space from some distance apart, meet and connect with each other. Decide why and how close the connection or contact is as the following scheme is played out.

- Run toward each other, pause about a metre apart.
- Accelerate an action, reaching out to the other, as if about to make contact.
- Slow the action down to slow motion.
- Reverse the action, retreating from the inevitable touch at double-speed.
- Resolve the action by returning to normal speed – finally making contact.

Observations:

- Can you keep each part of the scheme clear and accurate, even though the result will be perceived as one sequence?
- Can you see the impulse and arrival point of each part of the action?
- How does the sequence interact with the space?
- How do you keep focus if there is other ensemble action happening?
- Are the intentions clear within the abstract construction of the action?

Reflection:

- What did you observe?
- What would clarify the timing?
- Does using a metronome make the action clearer?

the slowed down action. For example, the main action might feel as if there are several speeds in operation, say 100, 120 or 130bpm, but the slow motion could have a uniform pulse speed of 60bpm.

Jump Cut

Effectively, this term refers to a jump in time and a rapid way to show that time has passed. It can create a strong sense of dislocation or fractured realism. It is essentially a very effective means to explore strangeness as the action moves forward.

Bullet Time

Bullet time refers to the manipulation of action to create unusual speed shifts within film shots. The term appears to originate from the technological ability of film to slow down time sufficiently to distinguish the action of a bullet being fired at a target. It was used in the Wachowskis' film *The Matrix* (1999) – an iconic work of contemporary cinema. This was done using the performers' movement, camera action within a shot, as well as in the editing. It is also a central mechanic developed for use in the action of video games, such as *Max Payne*, *Superhot* and its sequels. Use of this device, of altered time, developed from *The Matrix*, can create a sense of alienation and distortion that works well in live theatre. Steven Hogget, movement director, has used this feature to notable effect. He describes his use of bullet time as 'creating an action where an acceleration from normal time is used, then a slowing down of the movement follows, then the action completes, with a return to normal time'.

Freeze-Frame

As the terminology implies, the action can be chopped up in a *staccato* way, into equal lengths of a single second, as if the action were seen as separate, individual frames of film footage. This replicates the way the pioneer film-maker Edward Muybridge used film in the early development of capturing the moving image.

TASK: USING FREEZE-FRAME

Choose a whole-body work action that is in everyday or occupational use and clearly legible, e.g. chopping wood, lifting a heavy weight, folding bedding, digging the garden. Then, as if you had taken a series of single frame shots:

- Break down the action into short units of one or two seconds
- Clarify the impulse and arrival point of each segment of the action.
- Perform these units in the order of the original action.

Questions:

- What is the fixed time length of the action?
- Are the segments of the action clearly legible – with a clear start and finish – as it is broken down?

Reflection:

- How could this work in pairs or with a group?
- How does the *staccato* quality heighten the action and draw the eye?
- Assess the impact of the time device in relation to the narrative or script.

Rewind and Fast-Forward

This is using the movement as if the action was being rewound and reversed or, conversely, fast-forwarded. We use these actions regularly with moving GIFs or Boomerang clips on our smartphones, without a second thought, about the manipulation of single actions and the dislocation caused by the weird change of speed involved. It would be interesting to experiment with bursts of action using the same device and intersperse them with action at the expected speed and timing. In *A Dream Play* (1901) by Auguste Strindberg, in a version by director Robert Wilson for Stockholm Stadtstheater (2000), a movement section was created in which two women were collecting water from a pump involving realistic action of arriving at the pump, using the bucket, pumping water, handing it over. Robert Wilson then seamlessly reversed the action completely, starting at the end of the sequence. It gave an arresting, rather strange dreamlike effect, leaving us to figure out what had just happened as the movement was rewound.

In a dream. Performers: Elizabetta d'Aloia and Amir Giles.

CHAPTER 5

WORKING WITH DANCE FORMS

Dance, dance, otherwise we are lost.
Pina Bausch (1940–2009)

HISTORICAL DANCE AND A RECREATED WORLD

With a play or opera that is set in a historical reality, such as in a court or other context, a movement director can be asked to recreate a true semblance of history using dance. This could also be a regional or vernacular dance and community interaction typical of people dancing at an occasion that should be believable, in as far as it can be suggested for the characters and the plot. Research is necessary to examine images, paintings and accounts of the time, and for those to be re-imagined in relation to a script. To accompany this will be an understanding of social etiquette or behaviour appropriate to the time as action surrounding the dance. Belinda Quirey (1912–96) was a significant pioneer in early dance and its relationship to how footwear, corsets and the era affected how the steps read in manuals would be danced. The importance for her was to see the people with vitality, as living, breathing humans showing inconsistency and variety in how they danced.

the Pavane... described by Belinda Quirey as a 'dance of baffling simplicity', has to be understood in terms of the society and the beliefs that were in place at the time.... You cannot just take the surface of those dances – the movements are profound.
Jane Gibson in Movement Directors in Contemporary Theatre *(2020)*

In contemporary productions of, for example, Renaissance or Ancient Greek plays, the energy of the characters and their interaction may need to be addressed to reflect our own times rather than to recreate something that looks 'ancient'. This creative approach to a historic play can offer relevance to audiences of today, rather than present any realistic sense of historic accuracy. This type of brief means that the movement director must adapt material from one century and translate it into another. *Romeo and Juliet* could be set in Italy but in the 1950s, for example, or it could be interesting to interpolate the vitality of the clubbing scene within a Renaissance ball and how it can offer a contemporary urgency. It will result in a very different feeling from one of precise research into historical dance as recreated history.

Research and Preparation

Be aware that preparation on the era of the play, its context and location is essential. The movement director may be expected to have this knowledge at their fingertips. Here is an example from a rehearsal room at the National Theatre not so long ago. It was a new play, developed from a biographical account of a real figure, told in a documentary style.

OPPOSITE: **Jig dancer with the folk figure of the old English 'Obby 'Oss.**

Washer women dancing.

At the beginning of a full company call, early in the rehearsal period, and without prior discussion of a dance being included, the director suddenly asked

(and required an answer): 'What kind of dance would people have been doing in Berlin bars in 1925?' I took a breath and ventured, '...maybe a one-step? It's a ragtime dance from America. It might have been a bit early for the charleston to be danced widely?'. Whether correct historically or not, by the end of the three-hour call, the activity now involved teaching and arranging a one-step for almost the entire company. It was a dance I had learned two decades earlier when involved as a dancer in a TV programme on historical, social dances. Fortunately, it is simple and playful, and everyone had a great time. It became a moment that created atmosphere and reinforced the context of the play.

Recreating History

If the production is an accurate recreation of history, in as far as can be imagined, then it is important to establish at what occasion the dance takes place, along with the accompanying social etiquette of the era. We can see this beautifully done in recent films, which have a recreation of a social gathering that shows the importance of dance in Jane Austen's novels. In the *Playford Manual* of 1651, dances

The polka.

are accurately described with information on how the dance figures are to be performed. This work documented known English dances that were still in common practice in the early 1800s, as taught or perhaps 'called' by a dancing master. If the scene calls for 'Mr Beveridge's Maggott' then it is possible to recreate it. The etiquette and behaviour, such as greetings and salutations, leading the lady on to the dance floor and within the dances themselves, have been recreated by director of movement Jane Gibson, effortlessly and joyfully in the film *Pride and Prejudice* directed by Joe Wright (2005).

> *By approaching it from an actor's point of view, by considering their character carefully, you plant in their mind the idea that for everyone at that time, dancing was absolutely current.*
>
> Jane Gibson in Movement Directors in
> Contemporary Theatre *(2020)*

MOVEMENT CONSIDERATIONS NOT MERELY STEPS

The aim in teaching, recreating and using the material of well-known European social dances, is not to produce a competition-level performance of the material, but rather a sense that the dance is known material for a social occasion. A movement director arranges a dance and develops the material from the reasons revealed in the script and the director's vision as to why the dance is happening and its purpose within the play according to the directorial vision. It is often true that the movement director's knowledge of the dance form (whether through research or prior experience) will offer a great deal for the actors and directors to draw on. It is worth thinking about how important dances were to the social context and the world of the play.

> *Actors are often frightened of dances because they don't regard themselves as dancers, so you have to circumnavigate that by talking about the context of the piece and the characters they are playing, and by choosing movements that are simple, that they can really*

inhabit, they will be able to play their actions and objectives through the dance.

> Jane Gibson in Movement Directors in
> Contemporary Theatre *(2020)*

> *Most productions that I've worked on at the RSC have required a moment of 'dance'. I tend to frame these moments in my head like a dance party. The suggestions are either dancing at home in your kitchen, or you've just arrived at the party in your best outfit and your movement is as if like you are showing off your clothes or you're in the middle of partying at the club when the DJ is giving life, and everyone just seems to know how to do a dance at this point. This really helps me frame the feel of the dance and then you can pick and choose the steps or influences.*
>
> Ingrid Mackinnon in conversation on
> using dance in a play *(2021)*

Dance Experience

One factor for those with a dance background who become movement directors, will be working with actors and singers, trained very differently from dancers. Different dance heritages and technical approaches offer contrasting, yet related, experiences as body knowledge. It is worth considering the abilities and experiences of the company of performers with whom you are working.

What Embodied Experience is in the Group?

A contemporary dance training provides strength, alignment, use of weight and moving 'from the centre', with improvisation a key element. Ballet training as a classical art form embraces an aesthetic sense of line, as well as verticality, virtuosity, advanced skills of balance and control, with an unmistakeable sense of presentation instilled from a young age. South Asian dance forms have a classical heritage of stylized, structured narrative, rhythmic complexity and connection to spiritual roots. Afrocentric forms offer embodied rhythms central to the material danced with a connection to traditional roots and ritual purpose. Latin American traditional

Variety and difference on the dance floor.

dances offer a wealth of heritage combining dance forms from indigenous and imported cultural influences. In general, traditional folk forms globally have connections to festivity, ritual and ceremony. Urban forms such as street dance, arising from US popular culture, are now a mainstream activity, widely available as video clips on social media, with creative, competitive or improvised elements inherent to the form.

TRADITIONAL DANCE FORMS

Traditional dance implies something unwritten, not involving a choreographer, but instead handed down and carried out by a community, recognizable as a style and form of dance indigenous to a people or region. These dances live in the bodies of people and communities, and are expressed in the way they are shared in festivals, for seasonal or annual events and for ritual purposes. Traditional dance is not 'taught' as such but is acquired, learned or absorbed through the experience of dancing within communities from childhood. The way of using the weight, body carriage and the lack of presentational, performative norms found in the many European staged folk dance troupes is another very important aspect to differentiate. It is instructive

to watch an old man get up in a bar in the west of Ireland and dance a jig for his own pleasure, or a group of women in a square in Greece break into dance with its own song, forming a chain, or men in Bulgaria, dancing in a closely linked chain, with fearsome unison, at breakneck speed with rhythms that are complex and asymmetric.

Staged Dances

Almost all staged versions of traditional dances are not at all like this. As entertainment, timeless old dances are presented with the original tempi pushed much faster than in rural settings, and in costumes that are uniformly over-prettified. The arrangement and choreography are often over-drilled, verging on the spectacular, in a way that has lost all connection with the source material that the original dance might have been. If a play demands that type of presentation, then that may have to be the way forward. The spontaneous impulse to dance and express through dance involves improvisation, authenticity and inherent human qualities that have raw beauty in their imperfections. In staging dance, it is important to observe pleasure, focus and interiority in how a dance is danced, and embodies an experience that lies beyond words.

Dancing a czardas.

Dance and Music Migration

Dances and music migrate and are carried by people in their transience, crossing continents and finding new settlements. It was interesting to see in the play *The Jungle* at the Young Vic in 2019, that the dances of refugee migrants were brought to life by the performers and led by one of the actors, himself a migrant, who lived through the experience of the Calais refugee camp known as The Jungle.

In the UK, English folk dances are made accessible as a revival of old traditions through enthusiasts, practitioners and conservation by the English Folk Dance and Song Society. The ancient rural tradi-

tions of country dance, morris dance and jigs, dating back to before Shakespeare's time, have almost been lost by the effects of the industrial revolution and two world wars. This is true in much of Europe and they only survive in places where pockets of local dance traditions have not been entirely eradicated. In Hungary, the rich, rural dance traditions were kept alive in the cities through the pioneering developments in the 1970s, of the Táncház (dance house) movement. Musicians and dancers from villages visited and brought their music and dances to city dance halls on a regular basis, to share and hand on dance traditions to young people born in the city. In using folk forms it is worth being mindful of the distinct, stylistic principles held by a dance tradition. It is also valuable to observe how improvised elements are incorporated, rather than being fixed steps as set material. In traditional settings, individual performers offer both variety and difference as part of an indigenous style, just as is found in song and instrumental playing.

DECIDING ON A DANCE FORM

Discussion with the director, composer and designer about the country, region, context or setting of the play and the function the dance – social or ritual dance and its purpose – will determine the type or form for dance material, for example pair dance, chain or line dance, formal pattern dance or solo dance.

The decision about the references, source or basis for the dance material may revolve around whether the production concept is about updating or placing the work in a different era or recreating a historical reality. If a dance is mentioned in the script, is this right for the director's concept, the context and for the performers if it is a contemporary reading of the play?

Offer the director suggestions and be prepared to demonstrate, as well as show clips of, the dance material that would make a good starting place for the company of performers. It will be helpful to offer insight into the usual setting or context of the source to be drawn for the dance. For example, how it is accompanied, is it part of a ritual event, or does it take place in a dance venue and at what time of day. If a more technical or highly recognizable form, such as ballet, is required for the physicality of the play, it is important that the time for instruction and achievable quality of result is considered.

Research and Planning

In researching the dance form, look closely at the rhythms of the dances, use of weight, body focus and connection with others in the form itself. Written descriptions of dances help on form and sometimes the atmosphere of the dance, but don't reveal much about how the dances are done.

YouTube is a great resource, but be aware it is not always what it seems and it is not always reliable. If possible, find out more about the dance, its source and who is dancing it.

Ask yourself about the dances in relation to the production:

- Who will be dancing – as in which characters in the play?
- Will it be invented material, relevant in style and type to an existing form?
- How much time is available during rehearsals to develop the dancing with performers?
- What music is required and on what instruments?

Cultural Appropriation

In the use of researched dance material, it is necessary to be aware of cultural appropriation. What exactly is being researched in terms of social or cultural experience and how is that being airlifted into a staged version away from its original source? It may have ritual or sacred significance, which should not be ignored or undervalued. Within the world of the play, it is important to examine and respectfully acknowledge, with sensitivity, how the dance content will appear once removed from its traditional context.

Music

In the staging of dances, it is important to establish what music is required and if it is to be played live or recorded. If collaboration with a composer or music arranger is possible, then work with them; collaborate through the shared references of the specific music source and its instrumentation to develop the work, so that there are compatible rhythms and vocalization in the resultant work.

DANCE INSTRUCTION

Dance instruction can be included in warm-ups or given time in movement sessions. Teaching dance material to an entire company will create a resource for the actors to draw on as a known language that they can inhabit comfortably. This common language can then be used by the performers in a more oblique way to reveal connections and behaviour as aspects of the play. Improvisation using dance material allows for the physical imagination to connect as playful, heuristic investigation and discovery. The teaching and instruction can be formal and technical or use a less didactic, more creative approach, with improvisation frameworks that draw on the skills already present within the performers.

Learning and Absorbing Rather than Instruction

It is helpful to aim toward the material looking 'natural' in the body as if the performers had danced in this way often – and not just been taught some steps that they are trying to master.

The key fact about dances in their traditional setting is that they are done by people without any training as such. As an experience of dancing, this involves not learning steps from teachers but discovering a way of moving in a social or ritual situation and absorbing the style and material in its context. In some traditions, however, that have become theatre forms like flamenco dance in Andalusia, there is, of course, training and instruction, but in the Roma communities of Spain, the children learn from the handed-down practices and traditions of the community.

Improvisation

It is useful to use a stylistic framework for improvisation in which the performers can explore and inhabit material convincingly. It helps to think in terms of the principles of the specific form and then explore these with performers; for example, keeping legs low, staying grounded, swaying of the hips, stamping patterns, observing basic rhythms and accents. In pair dances, observe how leading and following occurs, and the relational purpose of the dance, as well, of course, of the context in the script or libretto.

Pair Dances with Improvisation

If we inspect the emergence of social dances, they all rely on knowledge of the form but are improvised on the dance floor and there are not always set steps. This phenomenon is found in the heady, turning pair dances of Eastern Europe, as well as Argentine tango, swing dance, jiving lindy hop and the jive. It is interesting how much improvisation exists within traditional and social pair dance forms.

Central European Dances

In the village dance houses of Central and Eastern Europe, the popular traditional pair dances, such as the Hungarian *czarsdas* or Romanian *învârtita*, have a similar use of several figures or phrases of material across four or eight bars. The couple in close embrace hold on to the tradition of man leading – woman following. The pair use the patterns and steps of movement, sometimes with swift turning figures, other times swinging the partner from side to side. A cycle of different dances continues throughout an evening to live music from a string band. The music can also be sung – for example, when musicians take a break. A dance cycle can include improvised male dances, a set of pair dances, starting slowly and developing to fast-moving, more intricate pair dances.

Tango

The idea of leading and following takes us into the mysterious and intricate world of the Argentine tango. The dance, with the pair in close embrace, has been described as 'walking to music'. The leading and following concept takes an experienced dance couple to navigate, as they move through a set of figures that give surprisingly equal opportunity

Waltz instruction in an actors' workshop.

for both dancers to have the freedom to improvise. It is worth remembering that in the origins of tango, it was danced by two men. In the twenty-first century, queer tango has made a significant impact on dance floors and in tango clubs. For research on the dance itself, it is worth visiting Sally Potter's black and white film *The Tango Lesson* (1997). She also appears in the film with partner Pablo Veron, and they capture the seamless flow and dynamism of the dance, reminding us of its compelling and enduring popularity.

Jiving Lindy Hop

This fast-paced early twentieth-century African-American dance form offers a loose-limbed polyrhythmic vitality, involving fast footwork and acrobatic pair material. In the film *Hellzapoppin* (1941) there is an electrifying five-minute lindy sequence, danced and created by the legendary Frankie Manning and partner Freda Washington at approximately the forty-eighth minute of the film. It is very athletic and includes many moments where the girl is flung across the floor and through the air. The relentless swing, push, pull, release and sense of momentum are captivating.

Formal Instruction
Using Ballet

In *A Dream Play* by Strindberg, directed by Katie Mitchell at the National Theatre (2005), a decision was made to use ballet as the main language of the play. This was a challenging choice, and to do this, a short ballet class was taught every day for forty-five minutes to the full company of actors. In the production, all actors wore long tutus at specific times, sequences were generated and a short passage from *Giselle* Act II was recreated. The aim was to regard ballet as a serious art, using its movement principles, not merely imitating steps or static poses. We examined the sensations found within the principles of classical ballet:

- Verticality, by using an uplifted torso and spine.
- Line, symmetry, using extended arms reaching through the upper back to the fingertips.
- Elevation as nimble, springy, small jumps in a devised sequence.
- Balance achieved by how a dancer feels connection to the ground.
- Lightness, embracing both poise and grace.

Using the Waltz

Movement considerations will dominate a movement director's approach to the waltz and, in particular, the rise and fall of weight with the balance of effort and relaxation in how a couple move together. The key to the waltz working well is leading and following. The

The feel of the waltz.

secret lies in what is embodied in the dance movement, rather than just the mechanical knowledge of the steps, and 3/4 time. While this is important, the waltz is a formal embodiment of attraction in a social setting. The close embrace of the waltz was an evolution and in social dance in court or formal settings was the only way in public that two bodies could be so close. Before the early 1800s, only folk dances in Europe were danced in close embrace. The waltz grew out of the ländler, a traditional Central European turning dance, also in 3/4 time, found at social gatherings.

In the waltz, the woman is held inside the frame of the man's arms. She can, however, retreat from him and entice him to lead as he sweeps her around the dance floor in a dizzying fashion. Far from needing to worry about what the feet do, the vitality of the dance is experienced through the sense of momentum, tension and release. There is a kind of elasticity in the connection found through the strong pull of the turning action. In a quick Viennese waltz, the rhythm of the music mimics the heartbeat. Take your pulse, note the tiny pause of the silent beat, and it can be counted as a fast three with the accent on the one. The three counts in the bar can be experienced as a 'one' with a sweep and a half turn, followed by the completion of the turn. The sweep and 'whoosh' sensation of a turning dance like this can be intoxicating. No wonder the waltz dominated Europe in the nineteenth century.

Afro-Centric Dance Forms

Ingrid Mackinnon writes here about her embodied dance heritage and dance experience, with its ritual and cultural significance.

Embodiment

Afro-centric dance forms have a significant and identifiable way in which movement is embodied. For example, in dances from Jamaica, there is a real connection to the earth and the soil, rather than to any refined patterning of footwork. The experiences of landscape, mountains and the ocean have their influence in the imagination of the people – and so, of course, does weather. When the sun comes out here in the UK, I just open up physically. I feel like a flower taking in the nourishing qualities of the sun.

European traditional dances were brought to Jamaica as a result of the Atlantic slave trade during the sixteenth century. The embodiment of these dance forms by enslaved Africans became the framework that influenced many traditional Caribbean folk dances, such as the quadrille and maypole dances. For me there is a sense of how meaning resides in the body, and a strong difference in embodied responses to music and rhythm between Euro-centric and Afro-centric dance forms and how melody is experienced quite differently between those two cultures. I think there's a real connection, because I've trained classically, in the most Euro-centric of forms, ballet, and in that I sense a real connection between the floor and carriage of the head. That sense of verticality, with connection through the floor upward through my spine, head and arms, is fundamental to that form of dance. However, in Afro-centric dance forms there is a key connection between the torso, belly and the pelvis, downward through the spine, to the feet and the ground. Perhaps, culturally speaking, dance forms that feel rooted in this way speak to my connection to the African diaspora through my heritage and culture. It makes me feel very at home in the Afro-centric aesthetic of dance.

Background

I tend to be energetic and to generate energy in others naturally. Dance forms from my background and ethnic heritage also produce a lot of energy. I think about the way that my mother danced in our kitchen or living room. Everything she did was over-the-top, even trying to do a limbo in the living room – she still tries to do it now and she's in her early seventies. She danced with lots of gesture, and the movement was very grounded and driven by the pelvis. My mother was not a trained dancer, but somehow her movements are connected to so many social dances that are found in communities of the African diaspora. The social dances from the early- to mid-twentieth-century period, like lindy hop and swing, really speak to me through the strong influence of

Grounded physicality.

jazz found in African-American vernacular dance. The dynamism of these dances resonates with my energy. Sadly, many of the African-American artists and dancers who are responsible for cultivating this lineage are not always noted or even given credit for influencing a generation of dancers and dance styles.

Connecting to Ritual Purpose

As I've gotten older, I've been more influenced by, and interested in, my own Jamaican heritage. My mother and her family feel the influence of Caribbean culture in the social dances and rituals that mark every stage of life. These appear as a feeling for the music and a communal expression in movement that would be done in Jamaica for a death, birth and healing, or any occasion in which there is a rite of passage. This goes back to the African origin of the enslaved people, and one of these dances is called the kumina. A rite begins with a kumina drum, which underpins all action, including song, solo dance and communal activity as both dance and song. There will be a solo movement gesture, an expression through the body that invokes spirits and ancestors to ensure safe passage home that everyone can slot into and it has a sense of repetition brought on by the percussiveness of the drum. There will be people dancing solo, but all connected through the rhythm. The beauty of it is that solo expression of an individual becomes woven into the communal expression as it becomes a group dance. Kumina can have two drummers or can just be one drummer and one dancer, or it can be several drummers, and maybe thirty dancers.

> *Kumina is a ritualistic medium through which African ancestors are celebrated and appeased. It's an art form combining dancing, singing and drumming, and has distinctive movements and cadences that make it easily recognizable.*
>
> From http://digjamaica.com/m/indigenous-religions-in-jamaica/kumina/ (accessed June 2021)

An example of a Kumina was staged by movement director Shelley Maxwell for the play *Nine Night* by Natasha Gordon (2018) at the National Theatre. The play follows a Jamaican family coping with grief when the grandmother of the family dies, and a traditional wake is held in a London home. For the 'nine night' ritual, family and friends gather over nine consecutive evenings to eat, drink and swap stories. There is a sense that the departing spirit presides, and on the final night is ready to leave home for ancestral roots in Africa to find peace.

DANCES IN PLAYS

Three Sisters (1900) by Anton Chekhov, Directed by Katie Mitchell, National Theatre (2003)

We decided to use the waltz as the key dance form that everyone in the company had been learning. It provided the vehicle for developing the major theme of unrequited desire in the play, as outlined by director Katie Mitchell. The idea for the improvisation we developed was a shared hunch that the physical attraction and rhythm embodied within the dance would reap rewards in addressing the theme.

The music used was the *Piano Quintet* (1976) by Alfred Schnittke (specifically the 2nd movement *tempo di valse*) as a reference for the actors. Schnittke's waltz is disturbing, with a fragmented feel to it, like snatches of memory. This helped in a sensory way as a musical metaphor for the theme of unrequited desire. With the director, an improvisation was planned in which the actors could explore the theme. Working together in a spontaneous, catalytic partnership, the structure for the improvisation was defined. A rule emerged: any performer could dance with anyone else. Chairs were placed randomly in the space, which allowed actors to sit out or join in, to dance alone or to follow social convention and request a dance.

The improvisation was extremely revealing about the characters and informed through a free flow of non-verbal encounters, which highlighted the theme of unrequited desire. The actors' engagement in the improvisation was a break-through in how the subtle tensions of the play could be revealed and, in my judgement, they carried this experience forward into the work. Whilst it did not result in specific material to be included in the finished work, it is one example of how a choreographic signature is present but embedded invisibly in the process.

> *From Melrose and Flatt, 'Finding and owning a voice', Dance Theatre Journal (2008)*

Dance work on *Three Sisters*, National Theatre (2003).

TASK: WHAT DANCE CAN BE RE-IMAGINED FOR THIS COMIC SCENE FROM *TWELFTH NIGHT* ACT I, SCENE 3?

SIR ANDREW AGUECHEEK: ... I am a fellow o' th' strangest mind i' th' world; I delight in masques and revels sometimes altogether.

SIR TOBY BELCH. Art thou good at these kickshawses, knight?

SIR ANDREW AGUECHEEK. As any man in Illyria, whatsoever he be, under the degree of my betters, and yet I will not compare with an old man.

SIR TOBY BELCH. What is thy excellence in a galliard, knight?

SIR ANDREW AGUECHEEK. Faith, I can cut a caper.

SIR TOBY BELCH. And I can cut the mutton to't.

SIR ANDREW AGUECHEEK. And I think I have the back-trick simply as strong as any man in Illyria.

SIR TOBY BELCH. Wherefore are these things hid? Wherefore have these gifts a curtain before 'em? Are they like to take dust, like mistress mall's picture? Why dost thou not go to church in a galliard, and come home in a coranto? My very walk should be a jig. I would not so much as make water but in a sink-a-pace. What dost thou mean? Is it a world to hide virtues in? I did think by the excellent constitution of thy leg, it was form'd under the star of a galliard.

SIR ANDREW AGUECHEEK. Ay, 'tis strong; and it does indifferent well in a dun-color'd stock. Shall we set about some revels?

SIR TOBY BELCH. What shall we do else? Were we not born under taurus?

SIR ANDREW AGUECHEEK. Taurus? That's sides and heart.

SIR TOBY BELCH. No, sir, it is legs and thighs. Let me see thee caper. Ha, higher! Ha, ha, excellent!

The text mentions:

- Kickshawes – something to imagine – that relates to the steps of the galliard.
- Galliard – a pair dance of Italian origin with showy material for the man.
- Coranto – a chain dance, with a hemiola rhythm.
- Caper – a leap.
- Backtrick – a somersault, perhaps, or tricky footwork.
- Jig – a solo dance in 6/8 or 9/8.
- Sink a pace or cinque pace – meaning five steps and refers to the galliard.

There is a sense of competition, humour, with bawdy references with the two characters referring to revels, as playful occasions for dance and celebration.

- What research might be involved to develop material?
- How could the dance terms or forms be re-interpreted for our times?
- Could a non-European form be used to interpret backtrick, caper or kickshawes?
- Make your own interpretation of the scene, using the skills of the actors to develop the playful banter of the scene.

A Doll's House by Henrik Ibsen (1879), Director Irina Brown, Birmingham Repertory Theatre (1996)

In Act II of the play, Nora begs her husband, Torvald Helmer, to coach her in a tarantella, which she will perform at a party. Nora wants to start dancing, needing his full attention and co-operation to distract him from going to the door and finding a problematic letter that is key to the plot.

> NORA. What are you going to do there?
>
> HELMER. Only see if any letters have come.
>
> NORA. No, no! Don't do that, Torvald!
>
> HELMER. Why not?
>
> NORA. Torvald, please don't. There is nothing there.
>
> HELMER. Well, let me look. *[Turns to go to the letterbox. NORA, at the piano, plays the first bars of the Tarantella. HELMER stops in the doorway.]* Aha!
>
> NORA. I can't dance tomorrow if I don't practise with you.
>
> HELMER. *[Going up to her.]* Are you really so afraid of it, dear?
>
> NORA. Yes, so dreadfully afraid of it. Let me practise at once; there is time now, before we go to dinner. Sit down and play for me, Torvald dear; criticize me, and correct me as you play.
>
> HELMER. With great pleasure, if you wish me to.
>
> NORA. *[Takes out of the box a tambourine and a long, variegated shawl. She hastily drapes the shawl round her. Then she springs to the front of the stage and calls out.]* Now I am going to dance!

From Project Gutenberg, online resource: www.gutenberg.org (accessed August 2021)

Questions arising about Nora and what to develop for the dance:

- What is a tarantella?
- Is this a dancing-master's version of the folk dance found in different parts of Italy?

- Or is it possibly the southern Italian woman's solo dance that is wild, earthy, extemporized and linked to the cult of tarantism, associated with the bite of a poisonous spider?
- From whom would Nora, a Norwegian housewife, have learned the Italian tarantella?
- In what way is Torvald Helmer qualified to coach her?

Given circumstances, a woman's social standing and dancing lessons:

- Nora perhaps had formal instruction from a dancing master with a cane, playing a violin.
- At the time, a woman could not be touched by a man she did not know. Corrections in the dance, such as stance or footwork, would have been with a touch of the cane.
- Would Torvald have accompanied his wife to the dance lessons, as she was not allowed to attend alone? He would also have paid for the lessons.

Solutions found in research and rehearsal:

- The steps used for the tarantella can be found in the *ISTD National Dance Branch Manual*, which offers a version of the dance, published around 1806.
- Helmer was given a cane to beat time and correct Nora with, so that he mimics the dancing master he has seen. The music was played through speakers.
- Nora has a wily objective to distract Torvald, by casting him as her dancing master and wanting him to correct her in the dance.
- As the dance progresses, Mrs Linde, her old friend, observes Nora as dancing wildly. This could enable a departure from the formal step patterns toward a wild, extemporized dance closer to tarantism, which can be found via YouTube.

Workshop on the jig from Shakespeare's time. Amir Giles and community performers, with Tim van Eyken on melodeon.

CHAPTER 6

MOVEMENT DIRECTION FOR A PLAY

All the world's a stage, And all the men and women merely players.

William Shakespeare, As You Like It *(1599)*
Act II, Scene 7

THE WORLD OF THE PLAY

This simple idea can mean many things in relation to a play script. The 'world' may refer to the narrative or ideas the script contains. It can also refer to the historical, social and cultural context in which the play takes place. It may be concerned with location of where the action is set and performed. Anna Morrissey, movement director, who studied anthropology before entering theatre, refers to the world of the play along with its acting company as 'being like a tribe'. I sense by this that she means the actors and how they inhabit, imagine and reveal the play as a story to be told. The idea of a tribe refers also to hierarchies, behaviour and whatever relationships may emerge between the characters. It can also refer to the psychological currency of emotions and intentions, differences and personalities within the actual situations in which they themselves, or into which, the author has put them. Beyond the script, there is much more than is on the page, which, not unlike the proportions of an iceberg, lies below the surface ready for investigation.

By navigating between the company of actors, the script and the director's vision for the play, a movement director creates the non-verbal language for this world. The director, as overall

Masked chorus movement.

OPPOSITE: **Jordan Ajadi in** *Puck's Shadow* **(2021).**

guide, will be searching and investigating with actors and the creative team the best way to reveal that world as it reaches out to an audience. Themes of the play once identified can form the foundation for all the work to be undertaken on the play by the creative team. Tone and style will become apparent as part of the director's portrayal of a play and how it is connected to the playwright's intentions.

THE SCRIPT

You have to approach any production as if you are working on the whole of the play, even though you might only be doing a particular section. Understanding the whole, and the director's intentions, is really important.

Ayse Tashkiran, Movement Directors in Contemporary Theatre *(Methuen, 2020)*

It goes without saying that the work with, from, through and around the script, dominates the rehearsal period of any play. This can include systematic analysis, creative exploration, a read through and detailed examination of the words, phrases and stage directions. All these processes will illuminate potential action, insight into characters and meaning in the stories to be told. The text itself offers much for the movement director to draw on that will relate to the body or groups of bodies in the play. It is worth making a close examination of the script initially for references to movement or dance. One crucial aspect is to establish if devising of a movement language for scene changes is required. This is a significant feature of many open-stage productions with scenes in multiple locations and no mechanical scene changes (*see* case studies in this chapter).

What is in the Script?

The script offers the playwright's straightforward division and breakdown of the scenario into the acts, then the scenes in each act. There may be a prologue and an epilogue or postscript. There is a list of *dramatis personae* or characters and within

the scenes are stage directions and information, which offer the playwright's suggestions for settings and action.

Director Katie Mitchell is detailed and systematic or, as she refers to it, 'forensic' in her examination of the script. It is scrutinized closely for information on details of place, location, time and ambience. The same applies to creating a precise timeline of action of given circumstances and all the known information for the character biographies. Director Femi Elufowoju Jr asks actors, before starting rehearsals, to read the play three times, and make three lists about the character they will play:

- All the things that the character says about themselves.
- All that the character says about other people.
- All that the other characters say about the character you will play.

Script Work

The emphasis of work on the script in the rehearsal room means that for substantial parts of the rehearsal period, actors and director sit down for 'table work' to investigate and share information and observations about the text and analyse the units or events in each scene. Working into the sub-text, drawing on the back story, defining the given circumstances, all provide clarity for the actors about the characters' intentions, feelings and actions to be played, and upon which movement work may be dependent. The process of how that works within the world of the play involves extensive exploration of the script to arrive at the richest and most informed result. Analysing a script is a very active and significant process for the actors and can involve a range of approaches, including making lists of attributes, to clarify information drawn from the text to reveal:

- Known facts in a character's life, with a timeline.
- Backstory of a character toward a biography.
- Intentions, thoughts and emotional states offered as character's 'action'.

- Given circumstances of specific scenes – time, place and prior activity.
- Events that occur within a scene.
- Movement potential for all these areas.

The dominance of the script work in the rehearsal room can mean that movement work is given less time. The important work of beginning to 'put the play on its feet' may involve improvisation as a way that the actors discover and respond to tasks and the possibility of action set up by the director. A more formal approach may be taken by the director using the term 'blocking', which is used to establish chunks of action, and events in a scene, which become fixed as the scheme of action. The director's work creates focus in the play, clarifying intentions and emotional content through action. Ideally, the movement director can feed into this work either in the room or in separate rehearsals or calls that focus just on movement work or fragments of dance material that will feed in to the whole later.

MEETING WITH THE DIRECTOR

Reading the script or source material before the first meeting is essential, as is being able to offer initial thoughts on how movement might be included and contribute to the production. The meeting will ideally reveal a lot about tone and taste, style and depth required, and will spark thoughts and strategies to offer. Movement director Natasha Harrison says that she arrives at the meeting with Pinterest boards, or YouTube clips and shares further visual material following up the discussion. By this means her use of terminology, planning, creative choices are made clearer and offer a source for deeper understanding and continued discussion.

Ideally, leave the first meeting knowing something about the director's take on the work and the questions raised regarding details on the world of the play or opera and the key characters. Other clues and information could include expectations in terms of the role of movement in the production and time needed to realize the movement work and

challenges envisaged. This will determine more detail about the director's expectations on the role to be undertaken such as:

- Further research and pre-planning required.
- If creating scene changes is to be part of the brief.
- The cast and the skills of the actors.

After further meetings, the brief for the movement work will become even clearer. Meetings with the designer and other creatives will inform about further detail of the concept, regarding visuals and style. As this is an organic, changing and evolving situation, further questions will inevitably emerge as ideas evolve and develop. Here is a checklist of questions following the meeting with the director to guide pre-rehearsal research or preparations:

- When is the play set? Is it to be held to an accurate, historical, time-period or updated to another era or even the present?
- What research has been done and what further is needed?
- What is the movement style or form as a basis to start with?
- How much time will be allocated to movement for the overall rehearsal period?
- How long can a warm-up last and is 'company building' part of the brief?
- What tasks for improvisation will need preparing?
- What will be invented language or draw on existing material?
- Is social dance material required and what is the music world?

RESEARCH

Based on discussions with the director, the research questions raised might go toward establishing if any movement sequences, without text, are to be created or if there are specific characterization references needed for certain roles. The movement work will involve translating ideas from the research with the performers.

Carrying out the Research

What does the research entail?

- Reading and analysing the script in detail.
- Perceptions of the body from specific eras or cultures.
- Art styles, specific painters or historic artists.
- Movement and style as dance material learned from a specialist in the field for accuracy.
- Literary research for descriptions of historic incidents.
- Culturally specific references in the play.
- Filmed footage, YouTube clips, film archives for specific footage.
- Photographic documentation or image galleries.
- Medical and scientific research into an illness or condition, either mental or physical, that is significant in a character or the world of the play.
- Practical, physical research as movement exploration on themes from the play.

Translating the Research

Decisions made before the rehearsal in the planning stages are vital. The clarity of the brief is the thing that gives the possibility of flashes of insight, which will come in the right measure...

Kate Flatt, Movement Directors in
Contemporary Theatre *(Methuen, 2020)*

The main objective is for the research to be effective in the studio as it is translated and developed with the actors. This entails imaginatively enabling movement material to be generated, morphed and re-configured through experiential tasks or activities. Tasks or improvisations can be set up, as frameworks, to continue the research as practice toward potential action for the staging relevant to any of the following:

- The context for the play, scene or activity performed by the actors.
- Movement references taken from a specific photographer, painter or sculptor.
- Music or dance form referred to the script, such as minuet, pavane, waltz, rumba, ragtime, shim sham and so on.

- Body knowledge and use as a physicality or style with the actors.
- The etiquette of a historical period.

Movement Tasks and Exploration

A movement director's tasks for improvisations can be a means to:

- Reveal themes of the play and aspects of them in specific scenes.
- Discover or reveal intentions.
- Find creative solutions with the actors.
- Find options that can challenge assumptions and reveal fresh approaches.
- Explore ways text can be interpolated with, or 'underscored', by movement.
- Examine how a theme from the script can be interpreted without text.
- Develop a sequence of action with or without music.

A variety of movement approaches on a play can be introduced to equip performers with specific skills as a common language of understanding for group sequences, which everyone in an ensemble can draw on. Heightened movement language and the skills to achieve it, such as slow motion or other time work (as referred to in Chapter 4), can be rehearsed with the ensemble. The action of the play may need stamina, with very fit-looking bodies or conversely very relaxed bodies. It is valuable to establish areas to be concentrated on in a daily warm-up. This may mean working on core stability for strength, aerobic material for stamina or ways of freeing and loosening up the body. A valuable strategy is to establish the terminology and repeated sequences that can effectively produce results.

Material Developed from Research

Power *(2003) by Nick Dear, Director Lindsay Posner, National Theatre (2003)*

Set in the court of Louis XIV, the play explores the ideas, events and intrigues around Louis XIV, the absolute monarch. The overwhelming autocracy of Louis XIV's reign has been well documented,

Louis XIV the Sun King.

regarding the rules on behaviour, status, salutations and order of precedence in court gatherings. Research centred on *Le Maître à Danser* (1775) by Pierre Rameau, translated by dance historian C. W. Beaumont. The descriptions of how to advance, retreat, remove a hat, to bow and curtsey, hand movements and appropriate deportment are illustrated and described. This historical record from the time calls to mind the certainty and correctness still to be found in the formal training and studio etiquette of classical ballet. A movement session was given for the cast on court etiquette in the court of Louis XIV. Material from this session was incorporated into the staging of the play to capture the formality, status, behaviour and etiquette of the court, the King and his courtiers. In addition, it served to provide clues for the actors on behaviour and character portrayal relevant to the script and plot.

Pains of Youth (1923) by Arthur Schnitzler, Directed by Katie Mitchell, National Theatre (2009)

Pains of Youth, set in the 1920s, is about a group of medical students. The script mentions Swedish

Swedish gymnastics.

exercises and a set of these was found on the internet, called Swedish Drill or Swedish Gymnastics dating back to 1910. These sources offered detail of the exercises, along with images of young women in gymslips demonstrating them. They indicated an interest in improvement posture, flexibility and mobility in young women and were clearly considered important for fitness at the time the play was written. I shared the exercises with the actors as background knowledge and information by incorporating some of them into the warm-up sessions. Although, ultimately, this researched material was not staged, the references had a bearing on the actors' entire physicality for the play.

Also in the script, during a dinner party, one of the characters (briefly) does a fragment of Javanese dance. The moment of the dance required the character to reproduce something they might have seen as Javanese material, possibly in a performance for a lecture demonstration, rather than reproducing in authentic detail, ethnic dance material, possibly of sacred origin. Film clips from YouTube proved helpful as a reference and the actress watched these for detail on the way of moving.

Ends of the Earth *(1996) by David Lan, Directed by Andrei Serban, National Theatre (1996)*

The script required a dance for a scene set in a Balkan tavern, with musicians playing live on stage. The character, a shady, local guy, was dancing a solo to authentic sounding music that was created out of fragments of a Serbian folk dance. Creating the dance involved research outside the studio, with the music director, to establish a Balkan rhythm of uneven phrases in 7/8 (sub-divided 1-2-3, 1-2, 1-2). Back in the studio, the dance was developed with the actor, so that it appeared as if it was part of his physical world with the movements natural to him. The dance involved rhythmic shifts of weight and a sense of him dancing for his pleasure not for others. The dance appeared to be spontaneous and a moment was found while he danced, to casually stub out his cigarette and then continue, gesturing to the musicians to play faster.

CHARACTER DEVELOPMENT

Actors and movement directors collaborate in finding movement elements in the form of behaviour, gait, stance or gesture that reveal the character by offering something that may arise out of improvised action and found material in rehearsal.

Three Sisters by Anton Chekhov (1900), Directed by Katie Mitchell, National Theatre (2003)

Solyony is the Lieutenant who falls for Irina Prozhorov, the youngest sister. He stumbles through the play in his gauche awkwardness, and his actions cause the death of Tuzenbach, who also loves Irina. The actor playing Solyony asked for movement help: 'I have to enter and do something with the intention to impress Irina' he said. Solyony's dance references could have been Russian dance, which is very athletic and impressive but beyond the skill set of most actors. With a working knowledge of Hungarian dance and thinking fast, an offer of a fragment of a Hungarian military recruiting dance seemed right. This involved a series of thigh and foot slapping, with clapping movements, using alternate legs. As it is not too complex to learn, he acquired the steps, their regular rhythm and became confident technically. He returned to the rehearsal room to work on the scene where this intention and action was needed for his encounter with Irina. In the scene, he entered, cornered Irina who had just arrived, exhausted from work, and enthusiastically launched into the dance fragment. The effect was both awkward and ridiculous. Exactly what was required it seemed, resulting in a gale of laughter from both Irina and the director.

Albert Speer (2000) by David Edgar, Directed by Trevor Nunn, National Theatre (2000)

Roger Allam played Adolf Hitler in the play *Albert Speer*, based on Gitta Sereny's book about Speer. In developing the portrait and body image of Hitler, Allam researched, from original film footage, the gesture language used in his speeches. The detail was immaculate and disturbing in its rhythm and intensity, as he performed this clearly recognizable

OBSERVING CHARACTER DETAIL – STEVEN HOGGETT, MOVEMENT DIRECTOR

The Curious Incident of the Dog in the Night-Time (2012), Directed by Marianne Elliot, National Theatre (2012)

Steven Hoggett speaks of how the movement director needs to be able release the physicality of the actor, to find the character and spot areas for development. The body can give away hints in rehearsal but also hinder development if over-thinking has held back the physical imagination from finding something revealing. The work is about making visible what we do as human beings.

Hoggett recalls sitting directly behind director Marianne Elliot and watching the action intently. Alex Sharp (as Christopher) was struggling in the scene where he is arguing with his father. He couldn't understand why his physicality felt at odds with his understanding of the physicality he had been using so far, nor could he line things up with what we knew from observing the physicality of autistic individuals. Because of the perspective Steven had, as well as studying and research we had been allowed to do by visiting a number of schools with autistic students, Steven was able to see the problem: 'Alex was using his index finger to point at his father. I noticed that it was completely straight and so the physical action was incredibly clear and assured. All I did was walk over and take Alex's index finger and made it slightly crooked, then asked him to complete the scene. The bent finger changed everything. The argument felt fluid and forceful but also had the qualities that Alex needed to feel secure in the role.'

The Glass Menagerie (1944) by Tennessee Williams, Directed by John Tiffany (2016)

Hoggett recalls working with the actress Cherry Jones who plays the domineering mother, Amanda.

> *Cherry Jones asked me what was going wrong, as she couldn't find her placement in the scene for a particular moment she had with the other actor. I asked her to let her left arm sit on top of the sofa. She did so, then looked over at me with a huge grin and said 'thank you' with her gorgeous Southern drawl. That one action genuinely unlocked the stalling block she thought might have been in the playing of the line and the scene. The clue was in making a conscious focus on a specific place in the body – the armpit – which created a bodily attitude that added a sense of Southern states' heat and authority, essential to the character.*

language with precision. The physical portrait he was creating was discussed and subtle ways to enhance his work on the body. In sideview, it was observed that his shoulder and upper back could be more rounded and the angle of the neck and head to the upper back be tilted upward. This revealed something more nuanced, making his stance less confident and more closed. Also explored was the way he turned to look at someone. It worked well if his eyes moved, as a separate action, before his head turned. This made his gaze alighting on someone else seem to come from a calculated thought with a sense of doubt and threat.

DRAWING OUT THEMES OF THE PLAY

Movement Director Ayse Tashkiran on *The Duchess of Malfi* by John Webster (1623), Directed by Maria Aberg, Swan Theatre, RSC (2018)

Director Maria Aberg proposed a strong idea for her production and described it as a play about a woman trying to survive in an extremely masculine world, in a world that is so masculine that it has become toxic. To that end, a chorus of men was woven into the production.

Duchess of Malfi – masculinity.

Working with a group of male actors, I set out to explore male military training as a way of building a movement vocabulary. The competitive element and weaponization of the body in the military were useful metaphors for toxicity. I researched first-hand accounts of Vietnam veterans for movement information about going through pain barriers and the pressures of existing in male-dominated hierarchies. I also researched the physiological and social impacts of PTSD common in war veterans. Endurance feeds qualities of invincibility and that, in turn, manifests as a sense of belonging. Military training prepares people to defend, fight, kill and die for others. Sports' training shares some of these qualities: endurance, competitiveness and training the body for a greater cause. Out of this combination, I created an abstracted movement sequence, which was effortful, muscular and sweaty. By the end of the play, this chorus became the group of 'mad men' that is used to terrorize the incarcerated Duchess of Malfi. By then their movement language was fragile, broken and incomplete. They too were victims of toxic masculine rituals.

Questions
In any sort of dramatic work, you are always looking for the push and pull of opposition. The question arose as to what is the lone female body in relation to this male chorus? In this play, the Duchess marries secretly, has three children, creates a cocoon of loving relationships within this overtly masculine setting. It felt like these contrasts were big, epic gestures that I could work with.

Physical Work
Carefully planned physical preparation with the chorus involved stamina training and running. I knew that sweating and visible effort would help us in creating this toxic, unfeeling, driven movement language. We were reaching for something that was fuelled by adrenaline and lacking in sensitivity, which smelt a bit like sports' spaces, and seemed to exclude other ways of being.

Using this for the Play
We decided from this work that the chorus who surrounded the Duchess would be all male and would go on a journey from a masculine, competitive sports' world, to an evocation of a militia to the 'mad men' at the end. The ideas are present in the text to a greater and lesser extent, but the research enhanced them. My research is always translated into do-able movement tasks for the rehearsal process. And in the end, this production had a significant movement language with a chorus of men in direct opposition to the female body.

Movement Director Kate Flatt – *Three Sisters* by Anton Chekhov (1900), Translated by Nicholas Wright, Directed by Katie Mitchell, National Theatre (2003)

The National Theatre production of *Three Sisters* (2003) by Anton Chekhov, directed by Katie Mitchell, had deeply considered use of psychological actions and thoughts of the characters contained within the events of the play. In the table work, the scenes were broken down into units and events in the narrative, and the intentions of the actors defined with precision and care. The four themes of the play as death, family, time and unrequited love were outlined.

Theme of Time
The theme of 'time' in Mitchell's interpretation of the play was heightened and brought out more

strongly by using slow motion. The brief movement sequences used for these surreal yet eloquent moments effectively created breathing spaces, and yet allowed the action of the play to continue seamlessly. The actors subtly slowed down their carefully examined action, taking it away from a normal, realistic use of time. As the movement director, I developed exercises with the actors, which examined the activity, but by using a metronome, the speed of the pulse, as beats per minute, was established. Working in this way, unified action was experienced by the actors and that was understood by all, as they made their individual pathways with movement at altered speed.

In this scene, it is winter and 20.00 in the evening. Masha, Tuzenbach and Vershinin are having a philosophical conversation about the meaning of life. Tuzenbach observes: 'Look, it's snowing outside. What's the purpose of that?'. In the pause following, the actors began to move in slow motion, in silence. Facing upstage toward the window, the movement included a turn of the head and upward, spinal energy from someone seated. One person stood up, and another took a few steps to look out of the window at the imaginary snow falling outside. Then, a few moments later, normal time action resumed. The stillness and softness of the action required control and focus on breath but was extremely effective for heightening awareness of the moment and drawing attention to the experience we all have when we notice that it is snowing. The unified tempo of the actors had a precise beginning and end of the shift in speed, along with subtle softness of dynamics in the action, but then continued seamlessly with the discussion in the scene. It was as if a collective thought became visible.

WORKING WITH SHAKESPEARE

The Body in the Text

Staging Shakespeare in the twenty-first century is not about recreating a distant history but recognizing how the stories, language and intelligence of the plays continue to speak to contemporary audiences. The theatre convention of his time included a masque with music and dance, and whenever music is referred to in the stage directions, there was also likely to have been a dance. To this day at the Globe Theatre on the South Bank, London, a jig is included at the end of a play, danced by the company, as was customary in Shakespeare's time. There is a lot to be discovered about movement in Shakespeare's extraordinary canon of work. Preparing to work on these great iconic plays and create a world relevant to our times, rather than re-create history, is the challenge for directors and movement directors. The language can offer a great deal for the movement director to explore as we can see in Ayse Tashkiran's account here.

Ayse Tashkiran: Script Preparation on Shakespeare and other Renaissance Plays

I have movement directed plays by William Shakespeare, as well as plays by other Renaissance writers, such as John Webster and Christopher Marlowe, at the RSC. My research and experience reveal that the plays all *feel* very different from each other and yet there is something in common in the mindset of the writers. This manifests in the way that the body is perceived and how that resonates in their language and imagery.

Mining the Script

When I read a script from the Renaissance period, I feel that I am reading *the body in the text*, because of the use of metaphor, dynamics and poetry. These help me to connect with an understanding of the union of soul, body and emotion of the time.

A non-specialist thought is that the language used gives you information about the body. A specialist movement thought suggests that the plays express an age of pre-modern anatomy and what was not yet known about the body. Even in our times, despite the understanding and discovery that contemporary science has given us about the body, there are still terrains of the unknown. The brain and the consciousness have large areas for exploration; even on a cellular level, discoveries are still being made. But the way that the body was perceived during the Renaissance is so different, it really jumps out at you from the text.

The Renaissance Body

Galen's influence was still percolating in a Renaissance conception of the body (Greek philosopher, physician, and healer, c. AD129–216) and the way that the body was articulated through the four humours. These are called phlegmatic, sanguine, choleric and melancholic, and reference early Western philosophy of medicine and human temperament. When you look for the humours in how the body is conceived, then you become sensitive to the sense of temperature, the connections between the organs, liquids and temperament. This is called undertaking a 'humoral reading'.

There are messages to the movement director if you read the text for mentions of temperature, the organs and body parts, along with other attributes of the humours. These were understood as red-blood – sanguine, black bile – melancholic, yellow bile – choleric and phlegm – phlegmatic, and all have their corresponding connections to the four elements of fire, earth, wind and water.

Rehearsal Preparation

Following from the script research, I make extensive lists, in the way actors and directors also do, of verbs and actions evidenced in the play. In my preparation, I list verbs and actions evidenced in the play. This informs my sense of the movement dynamic. I will draw up lists of everything that pertains to the body in the text. And then I create lists of environments, parts of the body, metaphors, patterns or animal imagery – anything that gives me access to the physical life of the characters and any potential movement action.

I don't necessarily talk about these lists with actors because they feed my preparation into the creation of exercises and tasks. They might inform the warm-up or creative movement sessions. Being methodical and detailed with the source material of the play, informs my direct approach toward embodied ideas. These are drawn directly from the text

and are informed by pre-modern understandings of physiology, contemporary neuroscience and anatomy. All three are layered together as I contemplate how to create movement-led work for the process of rehearsal.

Movement Director Ayse Tashkiran – *Romeo and Juliet* (1597), Directed by Erica Whyman, Royal Shakespeare Company (2018)

This is a play in which the heart is going to be the seat of love and violence, and for me raised the question, 'How can I prioritize the heart?' My approach was to start by activating the heart with the company through a specific warm-up journey. This takes us through all the technicalities of getting the body warm, and then into a physicality that celebrates free and communal movement and really raises the heart rate.

The benefit of doing this is that it enables the actors to feel like they have moved but also they can sense a change in themselves, in their bodies. Because of the movement activity, it means that they can feel temperature shifts and the quality of the skin change, along with the awareness of the breath moving and blood circulating. This warm-up and movement ritual brought me to a shared communal moment with the company, where we could focus on what I really wanted to develop, which was the connection between the heart and the hands.

Questions

In the party scene, Romeo and Juliet see each other for the first time and meet. The text suggests that they touch hands and lips – whether that's lip to lip or hand to lip or hand to hand – are decisions to make with the actors and director. The scene work involved looking at the relationship of how two teenagers might encounter. The language is sensual and laden with images of the body. What is the distance between them? Do they touch? What is the duration of touch? What does it mean to be under the gaze of family and friends? The movement director's preparation then takes a step forward as it starts to underpin a specific scene; in this case, incorporating the idea of the heart with lips and hands.

Romeo and Juliet.

Warm-Up Into Scene Work

The warm-up has many subtle and overt functions. One is to connect the actors in the company in an active way and to engage with each other physically. Once that starts to exist, then I might repeat the warm-up material with different flavours through the whole rehearsal period. For example, in *Romeo and Juliet*, the warm-up actually formed the movement language of the party scene. Once an embodied vocabulary has been introduced for everybody, you can then reintroduce it when doing scene work.

Movement Director Jonathan Goddard – *Timon of Athens* (1606), Director Simon Godwin, Royal Shakespeare Company (2018)

Preparation

Timon was played by actress Kathryn Hunter in this production. She says, before the banquet scene, to the assembled lords who have betrayed her:

> *Most smiling, smooth, detested parasites, Courteous destroyers, affable wolves, meek bears, You fools of fortune, trencher-friends, time's flies...'*

Timon makes references throughout the play to dogs, beasts, as well as wolves. In preparation for working on the show, I discussed with director Simon Godwin how it might be useful to explore the idea of pack mentality for those ultimately treacherous to Timon. The movement work I explored with the actors informed many moments throughout the play, most visibly in the banquet scenes where I worked with physicality, action and time to create a useful and visceral language.

Practical Research

I found video references of wolves in the wild and chose clips I found interesting that might provoke discussion. I played them for the actors and encouraged them to talk about the characteristics that they saw. For example, how wolves hold themselves, sit, stand, change direction and how they notice things.

First, we discussed what we could see, then we talked about sensory aspects – how do wolves listen, smell, touch, interact with objects and each other. After that we narrowed things down to four or five physical ideas that everyone agreed on. There might be a decision, for example, that everyone could be hearing or listening from the side. I find it useful to start with four or five clear ideas to explore, so I can see how they might be of use in a group movement language. This also helped with the pack mentality and moved us toward an exercise with Timon as a pack leader, and the ensemble following Kathryn Hunter's instincts and timing and becoming like a Greek chorus.

Timon of Athens – wolf pack.

Physicality

We worked on the feral qualities we found from the study of the wolf. I try to encourage actors to find movement as something that is happening to the body, rather than something that you are doing as an action. I ask actors to observe changes that are internalized and happening within, as one might notice the weather change or the aches and pains of a cold beginning to manifest in your body. I prefer this approach to that of proactively trying to perform or portray movement, and I encourage actors to listen and let the idea perform them. We used the approach of a sliding scale, with ten being wolf and one being human. We then looked at the material and action we had already found and explored switching between these numbers as a way of becoming familiar with the movement language. From this exercise I was then able to conduct the action for the banquet; for example, with everyone using a common movement language.

Using Music

In my rehearsal sessions I like to work with sound. I prepare a playlist in advance that has the right feel for the action and work. This could be anything that I feel has the right atmosphere and tone, not always music, and sometimes I might use natural sounds like birdsong. This can be a change for the actors from working only with text and provides a different stimulus.

Time Work

I developed ways with the actors of accessing abstract uses of time. I wanted them to be able to move fluently from one quality to another. For the banquet, we wanted to give the sense of it lasting many hours but with all action condensed to only a few minutes – like time-lapse photography. I worked on the abstract qualities and shifts in time that would be useful to us during the warm-up, so that they could be used as a common language. Some parts of the banquet we decided should be done at a slower speed; for this I asked the actors to move as if in a swimming pool and to think about how the limbs are supported in, and by, water. Other parts of the scene we played with suspension in time

and fast-forward actions to accelerate the visual picture, quick jumps from one tempo and ways of moving to another. As the work developed, I was able to 'conduct' these shifts in rehearsals by using a cymbal, which when struck had a resonant sound that evoked the quality of change that I was looking for. I found the instrument more useful than a clap, which was too sudden or swift, it meant the changes of action evolved in a way that had a quality shared by the group and a unified dynamic. The composer picked this up for the score. I try to remember that the actors still have to act, so within any scheme I devise, I aim to keep material structured but loose, which means I can conduct any 'machinery' of the time factors within it, as the scene unfolds, and still allow the actors to be playful and free.

MODERN AND CONTEMPORARY PLAYS

Movement Director Sarah Fahie – *Endgame* by Samuel Beckett (1957), Directed by Richard Jones, Old Vic Theatre (2019–20)

The world of *Endgame* presents challenges for both the director and movement director, and for this production we felt it needed joint research and preparation. Richard Jones and I spent five days across three weeks, then had two-hour online meetings every week for a further three weeks. With Richard I went through every 'action' (as in thought or psychological intention) that would affect the activity of the characters. This gave us a shared, agreed understanding of the world of the play as a place from which to proceed. This process enabled us both to work out the activity of the characters, which included the pauses written into the script. We also looked at how disease appears in the play and brought in a back story, which referenced the emerging pandemic of Covid-19.

Beckett's Instructions

Beckett gives very precise and detailed stage directions in the script, which are not unlike a recipe. The opening page alone gives full details of the initial activity of the character Klov and establishes the fact that the main character Hamm doesn't move from his chair throughout the work. Action is delineated and described by Beckett using the precise shape and dimensions of the set.

Beckett and Vaudeville

The world of *Endgame* requires that any movement within it not only follows Beckett's precise stage directions and instructions, but also references the comic work of vaudeville, involving slapstick and clowning.

In order to develop the work from this perspective, Mitch Michelson, an expert on comic business in music hall style, attended some rehearsal sessions to give advice.

Given Information

- Hamm – is unable to walk and commands from his throne-like chair, blowing a whistle to summon Klov his servant from offstage. The character used fake legs, wasted from lack of use.
- Klov – has ritualized activity throughout and is starting to suffer with poor eyesight and has spondylitis, gradually making him more bowed. His walk becomes stiffer during the play. He does not like to touch or be touched. His body is pulled into ritualized action as he enters the stage using defined paths, summoned to work for Hamm. He manoeuvres and climbs a ladder.
- Nagg and Nell are two characters who only appear by popping up in two dustbins, with their legs not visible and from which they don't move.

Further Research

Richard and I looked at *Quad*, an earlier play of Beckett's directed by him for television in 1981 (available on YouTube). The play is without words, only movement, and takes place in a square set. This short, austere work uses a square of flooring, with entrances and exits only at the corners of the square to establish geometric paths. The performers obey precise, inherently musical instructions, with variations in speed. They appear to wear a path, relentlessly, into the square on the floor, creating a 'grey tension' and 'machine-like precision'. This was exactly

Endgame – the ladder.

the effect we wanted for Klov's ritualized activity, his entrances, exits and pathways through the set.

Movement Challenges and Construction

Klov's character (played by Daniel Radcliffe) has enormous amounts of movement throughout the play. He not only has to climb the ladder he brings on, but also manoeuvres it with some dexterity and at speed. This meant that every move for Klov, including the ladder moves, pathways, entrances and exits, had to be carefully constructed with rhythmic precision, observing the limitations given in the spatial aspect of Beckett's stage directions. Klov's movement for climbing the ladder had to be created, almost like a dance. It involved fourteen movements to climb – using the seven rungs – and these needed to be consistently rhythmic and get faster during the play. The focus on the movement for the actor playing Klov, and my work with him, was to keep the material accurate rhythmically, especially with regard to speed.

Movement Director Anna Morrissey – *Emilia* by Morgan Lloyd Malcolm (2019), Director Nicole Charles, Globe Theatre (2019)

The play explores the unheard voice of Emilia Bassano, reputedly the dark lady of the sonnets, and a muse of William Shakespeare. In addition, by working with the outreach department at the Globe, the work was furthered by a group of students who became part of the creative exploration process. I found it incredibly useful to create material with them and 'get it on its feet', as well as look at it within the Globe theatre playing space and in the context of the story.

Finding the World of the Play

I was inspired by the tone of the writing, which was not at all a straightforward historical play. As a contemporary play, it does address the historical references but also embraces a contemporary vernacular. Emilia Bassano, as a real person, does not have a documented history, so the play and its staging explored giving her the voice that was denied to her in her lifetime.

There also emerged an interface between three major strands:

- Historical truths and known facts; dances of the time and the characters.
- Contemporary politics and language and the interpretation of them but in our time.
- The epic, mythical concept of the muse, which Emilia was, explored in the movement of the chorus.

Research and Development

In the making of Emilia, I was part of early discussions and thought processes involved in the research into the era, the world and the woman herself. There were three separate periods of studio research and development, which were mainly designed for script development and what the play would become. From the first draft, I could see that a lot of sequences of movement throughout the play, with different degrees of complexity, would be needed as they became written into the script.

We asked ourselves, 'What does the concept of the royal "court" mean to us now?'. Emilia goes to court in the play, and we explored the dances and world of the court and how we could interpret that for her and show facets of her character. This meant understanding the galliard, pavane, la volta and the coranto, all dances mentioned in Shakespeare and common knowledge in the court of Elizabeth I and James I. Because the Globe Theatre was new to me, I was glad I had previously been able to study and work with Glynn MacDonald, Master of

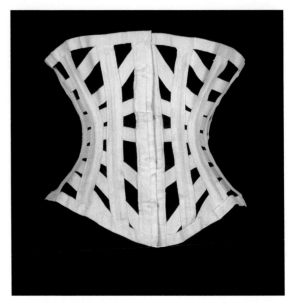

Corset from the Royal Worcester Corset Company (1864–1950).

Movement at the Globe Theatre, London. She was very informative and helpful about working with the challenges of the Globe as a playing space. I was also able to feed this work into the writing of the play from the perspective of Renaissance dance and its importance as social activity at the time Emilia lived.

In the Studio

I was able to take over the third studio research period and explore the movement aspect more fully and see how it could develop within the play. I am glad of that, as time became an issue once we were in full rehearsal. This enabled the writer, director and I to see how it could work. It was an extremely valuable time. I was able to reject things that didn't work in the open, daylight space and also discuss what we would keep. The conversations that took place became supportive and enabling as creative collaboration and in having confidence in the production it would become.

Politics of the Corset

Throughout the history of the corset being worn it has made a significant contribution as a powerful restraint, both bodily and political, to the containing of women. As part of the development of work on the play, I tried on an original whalebone corset and experienced the restrictive horror of it. Research into the wearing of a corset indicates that it caused not only restriction of breath and fainting, but was also a significant agent in the actual loss of women's ability to speak and having the space to speak. This resonated also in an artistic sense, with Emilia finding her creative voice as a freedom for herself and other women. It became a potent metaphor for us, in what it feels like to be restricted and the meaning of that in a political sense. It led to thinking about, and working with, the sensation of being contained and released, plus the movement associated with those opposites. However, I am glad to say that corsets developed and adapted for stage use in contemporary theatre are kinder to the body, making movement and use of the voice more possible!

Rehearsals

During production rehearsals at the Globe, there was only one rehearsal space, so time to explore was not in great supply for movement rehearsals. This meant, with pressure of time, I had to make a lot of work directly on the performers, with material pre-prepared and taught. It was a very fast rehearsal process with rehearsals from 11.00 to 17.00 every day to stage the play. In that time, I created eleven movement sequences, plus, in keeping with the tradition of the Globe Theatre, a final celebratory jig. This was made with the ensemble and was explored to a specific purpose from improvisation, using an accumulation exercise of dance steps, developed in response to the final speech.

Movement Director Diane Alison Mitchell –
***Our Lady of Kibeho* by Katori Hall**
(2019), Director James Dacre, Stratford
East, Royal and Derngate (2019)
Background to the Play

In Katori Hall's play, the script is based on the true story of young women in Rwanda, who, in the early 1980s, had a vision of the Virgin Mary, which predicted the awful violence and tragedy of the genocide that was to happen in Rwanda in 1994. The world of the play presents a complex set of areas to understand and take on board. The director shared extensive background information, both visual and in literature, pertaining to real-life accounts and incidents in the play, which were also placed around the walls of the rehearsal room.

My Background

I think, as a movement director, you always bring your own experience to the work at hand. Through my African-Caribbean heritage and experiences in dances of Nigeria, Ghana, Benin, Guinea, Republic of Congo, South Africa, Jamaica, Haiti and Cuba, I was able to draw on rhythms and aesthetic principles of undulation and pulsation that recur and can find their way into productions. This creative practice and how I look at the body informs my process with a sense of grounded movement, percussive music and embodied rhythms.

Research into the Play

I began my research looking at the body in Catholicism and in the iconography. I then placed that information back into Rwanda, Africa and African Catholicism for the context of the play. When I began working physically, I realized it always comes back down to the bodies of the people and my research turned toward Rwandan heritage and its dances. I particularly investigated the Rwandan women's dances, and their rising, sinking, fluidity and undulating head, arms and torso as a celebration of the feminine. I took those dances back to the context of the body in Catholicism, along with the idea of being 'taken' or visited by the spirit within Christian practices that are rooted in Africa or throughout the African diaspora.

Katori Hall's script uses words such as shiver, quiver, convulse, and each required a different physicality to interpret them for the movement development. I explored how the visions referred to in the play happened and how spiritual experience can be expressed and along with that the risk or cost to the person who is visited. This movement work became a juxtaposition between the fluidity and grounded lightness of the dances and the physicality of spirit visitation.

Process

The extensive research around Catholicism I had done provided valuable information, but it was important to filter that back through my own experiential knowledge. It is in that meeting between all of the research, how you are handling it, reimagining and channelling it that draws together the different facets. These can be from your own individual experience or specific to the research into the context and world of the play. I think that it is at the heart of my creation process and the journey I go on with the actors. The actors then are actually living and embodying all the preparation and taking it forward within their own process, inhabiting the character in the world of the play. It is these multiple processes between the creatives and cast, overlapping and intertwining in a symbiotic cycle, where the alchemy occurs.

Collaboration

There were a lot of creatives in the team on *Our Lady of Kibeho* all feeding their work into the whole. I recall being in a room with magic consultant John Bulleid, sound designer Claire Windsor, aerial specialist Vicki Amedume, music director Michael Henry and the composer Orlando Gough. At times we might all be working on the same scene at the same time along with director James Dacre. For example, I would work with two people, James would be over there with others, Orlando would have a keen eye

Young African nuns.

across the whole landscape of sound and action; Vicki on aerial sequences and Michael would be with two people at the piano. Out of that came rich, creative, follow-on discussions where we would share the findings and developments, and feed off each other's creative input in response to the emerging work. After inspecting the mechanics and ideas, we would get everyone back, all together, and move forward. It was challenging, but really exciting.

Movement Director Lucy Cullingford – *Constellations* by Nick Payne (2012), Directed by Michael Longhurst, Duke of York's Theatre (2012), New York (2014), Donmar Production at Vaudeville Theatre (2021)

Constellations follows Roland and Marianne through their romantic relationship. The play refers to cosmology, quantum mechanics and the belief that there are multiple universes pulling people's lives in various directions. This is reflected in the play's structure as brief scenes are repeated, often with different outcomes and involve time shifts. Marianne learns that she has a brain tumour and has less than a year to live. The setting was an open floor, with no set elements or furniture in it. The design by Tom Scutt had white balloons suspended above and at the back of the stage, offering a sense of impermanence.

Unpacking the Play

I came on board to work on the play just before we started the rehearsal period. As a new play on an open stage with no props, the director was keen to engage a movement director as part of the creative team in order to help explore the physical dynamic between the actors and the specific demands of the ever-shifting universes. In the early days of meetings and rehearsal, my job involved unpacking what the movement language might become alongside the other creatives. I worked with Michael Longhurst on the different, finite intentions behind every transition, interrogating the entrances and exits of every scene, in collaboration with the actors. I began by exploring a fairly open movement vocabulary with the actors looking at ways they could access physical tension along with shifts of level as action in the space and body – we began to evolve a language rooted in shifts of tensions through time and space and connected to the finite intentions within the scenes. A framework began to develop.

Movement Landscape

The movement work specific to *Constellations* became about the actors navigating the emotional energy, across space and between each other. At the heart of the play are the quantum physics references. As the narrative was not a linear path, it was crucial to discover in the structure how they could jump easily into each new section and the various movement interventions that punctuated the play.

Emotion and Tension

The key aspects that emerged were connected to the degree of emotional and physical tension involved: the shifts of level, energy and emotional narrative in time and space necessary in driving the action. It was important for me to thread Laban tools and influences into the work (I can't remember if I told the actors). It became an essential aspect in warm-ups for the actors to access different types of physical tension as useful to their roles. They needed to locate this as both heart- and thought-led action, as they navigated an open stage.

Geography of the Space

Locations of the play had to shift, even though we were on an open stage. For us all, it became about creating a reality out of an imagined space. We worked with these questions: Where are you? What can you see? What is the geography of the room? What is on your horizon? What's the time? What is around you? What is the intimacy of this space? Where is the sofa? Chair? Ballroom-dancing teacher? Where are the other named people in the space? This fed and made a difference to the evolving movement work.

Time and Reality Shifts

A further consideration was whether the movement elements would be with or without text or a blend of both. The bare stage enabled a greater sense of abstraction in the movement and asked a lot of the performers as they navigated the emotional landscape of the piece. There was, overall, a sense of being on a dance floor. In one of the shifts, they end up doing a ballroom waltz (as the pair go to a dance class together). The element of the ballroom helped to form a basis for other aspects of the movement language also; such as atoms, molecules knocking against each other, body language, a first meeting, the arc of the relationship and how the characters literally had to dance around each other. Sometimes meeting in harmony and sometimes being torn apart, fractured or just missing each other.

Transitions

The transitions between sections, in terms of action, places and time, started off as being very lengthy. We started with making a transition from one state of physical tension to another over about ten seconds. But as rehearsals progressed, the actors could navigate their way through faster emotional shifts, and a sort of choreography of emotion emerged.

The Experience

I found it a deeply moving and compelling experience to create for this. As theatre, the movement dimension lay at its very heart and was fully integrated within the production of the play and woven into the actors' rehearsal process.

Passage through time.

CHAPTER 7

MOVEMENT DIRECTION IN OPERA

The opera world is a machine with many levels of expertise.

Sarah Fahie, Movement Director,
in conversation (2020)

WHAT IS INVOLVED?

Opera is a form of theatre associated with a significant, historical canon of classical music. International opera houses across the world enable large-scale productions and currently instigate new versions of well-known works within state-subsidized companies or supported by high-profile, corporate donors. Grand opera is dramatic, often intensely emotional, with rich narratives, famous arias and duets, which in performance are accompanied by a full orchestra and chorus. In addition, there may be actors, dancers, children and specialist performers (acrobats, pole dancers, fire eaters, bungee wire performers and so on), all making for complex rehearsal logistics and demands in terms of technical production and stage management.

Productions offer highly visual concepts that involve integrated movement and action, large-scale sets and lavish costumes. New productions of older works, with a director's concept, can aim to make an old story relevant for contemporary audiences by staging in a contemporary context and modern dress. Toward this end, the value of movement direction work in opera is immense. Movement direction can be instrumental in generating fresh vision, with a musical score written in a very different era. The expertise of classical musicians, opera singers, the chorus, *repetiteurs* and conductors, in terms of how opera is produced and performed, cannot be underestimated. The different components of this undeniably complex machine will all have a bearing on the movement director's work and the necessary interaction with music in this context. It is a very different genre from text-based theatre-making.

WHO IS INVOLVED?

The Conductor

The conductor, as lead artist, has a highly responsible job, to recreate the music for each performance by holding together the orchestra with the onstage the singers and chorus. A successful conductor communicates what is required through their own expressive movement, which will dictate tempi, quality, volume and feeling they want from the music. As creative individuals, they can produce speeds or tempi in performance that can vary considerably from that with the piano in the rehearsal room.

The Director

The director on a revival or new production will have one, possibly two assistant directors, who will document the production staging and be responsible for the schedule, planning and the important preparation of understudies for principal roles. It is important to work sympathetically and supportively with them. The director's concept for the staging of the opera, ideally, goes hand in hand with the musical interpretation of an opera score by the conductor. This entails significant collaboration and decisions

OPPOSITE: *Peter Grimes*, **directed by Phyllida Lloyd, Opera North (2006).**

about cuts in the score of specific passages that are surplus to the needs of the staging. Once decided, the cuts of repeats, bars or sections often are discussed with music staff and marked into the score, and then distributed to all parts of the music department and, eventually, to the orchestra. Cuts often of non-sung parts of the score will undoubtedly affect movement work and will need to have been discussed and understood in advance.

Music Staff

Musical preparation precedes and continues throughout the staging rehearsals. The conductor is aided by a specialist team, including an assistant conductor, a *repetiteur* at the piano and a chorus master or mistress whose sole job is to rehearse the chorus music in the repertoire. It is expected that opera singers will arrive at staging rehearsals knowing all their music and lyrics. They will possibly be singing in a language not their own, and a language coach will be at rehearsals to check that pronunciation is correct. All rehearsals will be accompanied by a pianist, who will need to know, and be consistent with, tempi established by the conductor. It is rare to use recorded music (which may not be at the right tempo) for movement material or sequences for non-vocal passages.

OPERA REHEARSALS

To produce opera for stage performance, there are notoriously tough time-constraints and intricate scheduling demands for all concerned. It is significant that opera houses plan very far ahead – two to three years in some cases – and decisions on casting, scheduling and creative artists' availability are made well in advance of rehearsals beginning.

There can be availability issues for rehearsal if there are star singers who work internationally and arrive for very few rehearsals. It can mean that they offer limited time for rehearsals of not only a revival of an older production, but also for a new role. It is advisable for the movement director to attend the *sitzprobe*, which is a full rehearsal for all involved but with no stage action, only the singing of the

full opera with the orchestra. This is always an illuminating moment in the process.

Studio and Stage

The staging of a new production will require the team of director and movement director to collaborate fully with forward-planning for the rehearsal period and acknowledge the scheduling challenges, which are managed by the administrative department, assistant director and stage management. The movement director needs to be aware and understand the process and the expectations involved. In general, movement rehearsals will take place in a different studio, sometimes off-site.

Stage rehearsal time can be limited, as it is shared between production rehearsals with piano, which are led by the director, and orchestral rehearsals, led by the conductor with focus on the needs of the music and the singers. Stage rehearsals for the movement director afford a good time to see how the studio work looks, but will mean limited time to create anything new, or sort out problems arising from any restaging that may be required.

It is important to note that in opera there is no period of 'previews' as is normal when working on a play or musical. A full audience is invited to a public dress rehearsal, but there is no further rehearsal time following it and only a 'notes session' for the creative team to speak about anything that might be problematic.

Score Reading

The score is the bible of the opera being worked on. It is best if the movement director arrives at rehearsal being able to navigate their way around a piano score. For a long opera, this can be in two volumes and quite heavy. Italian terms and figure numbers in the score are referred to and provide a shorthand by which the musicians and singers know from where they are going to start. Figure numbers indicate the start of a section and a precise tempo as a metronome marking, as well as dynamic qualities in Italian, all need to be understood. A crash course in music theory is extremely helpful to know what is meant by an instruction from the conductor, such as 'Can we go back to the *ostinato* please?'. Actors, dancers,

Damnation of Faust, **directed and designed by Yannis Kokkos, Chatelet Theatre, Paris (1990).**

movement artists or other non-singing performers in the studio, will need your help to know which bit of movement material they are starting with. When creating movement sequences, it is helpful to mark sections in the piano score where specific instruments feature, so that performers can listen out for them once the orchestra arrives.

OPERA SINGERS

Singers are musicians and vocal artists who have been trained so that their natural voices can carry across the orchestra pit. Their voices are not amplified by use of head microphones as in musical theatre. A large orchestra has as many as sixty musicians and produces a powerful sound. Training prepares singers for the famous and iconic works in a repertoire of well-known audience favourites by Verdi, Puccini, Rossini, Bizet, Wagner, Tchaikovsky and Mozart. What these singers can do, and accomplish in solo,

duet, trio or quartet passages, is astounding from the point of view of vocal talent, expertise, musicianship and technical accomplishment. The musical repertoire is demanding and requires vocal skills honed over many years of training, coaching and practice.

International Opera

Star billing is given to international stars who attract audiences for the extraordinary calibre of their voices and their interpretations of specific roles, and legendary status gained through recording contracts, as well as live performance. It is likely that stagecraft, acting and movement ability will have been acquired through studio experiences and working with directors in opera houses worldwide. It is still usual practice for international opera stars to arrive quite late on in the rehearsal process, knowing the music, but attending only one or two studio rehearsals to learn the action before the stage rehearsals take place.

Trust and Support

Patience and tact are needed in developing a relationship of trust, if movement and dance are to be a significant part of a role in the opera staging. There can be challenges in terms of experience, levels of fitness, body shape and confidence with acting. It is worth recognizing that these performers travel to work in diverse, new situations all the time. As stars they can also 'call the shots' and be both demanding and uncompromising with director and movement director alike. However, to be in the studio with a great, international artist can be an illuminating encounter. It is a privilege to work with the skill, talent and professionalism of great singers such as Sir Thomas Allen, Christopher Purves, Roderick Williams, Sir Willard White, Anna Netrebko, Dame Josephine Barstow and Lise Lindstrom. As singers, these performers are equally at home with stage action or movement, and act convincingly, with ease, in all aspects of the role and portrayal.

IN AN OPERA REHEARSAL ROOM

As a movement director in opera, it is usual to find yourself working in a studio with a barrage of desks and tables at the front of the room, behind which are conductor, director, assistant director, music staff, language coach and stage management team, all with the score in front of them; there is no intimacy, even if a tender love scene is being rehearsed. Here are some examples of what might be encountered in the rehearsal situation.

Example 1 Grand Opera Rehearsal

- There is a rehearsal for a soprano and tenor, both of whom have international careers and who have just got off aeroplanes from different parts of the world. Italian is their common language. This will be their only day of studio rehearsal before stage rehearsals with the full cast and chorus on the following day, for a first performance next week.
- The scene requires the movement director's help to make a loving embrace of a passionate nature

work successfully between the experienced, yet nervous singers, who have only just met.
- It is hoped that they are willing to cooperate and do not want changes made to the staging, such as demanding to be closer to the conductor, or even wanting to do what they performed last year, in some other opera house.
- The movement director's challenge is to help them to manoeuvre their (rather unfit) bodies into a convincing, graceful embrace that starts with a kiss and ends with them lying on the floor, showing desire and passion. The singers are concerned about being able to see the conductor for vocal delivery with the orchestra.
- The movement director begins work, but the stage manager announces to the room that there will be a tea-break in five minutes time and afterwards the director would like to move on to another scene. This means rehearsing the action within a time constraint.

Example 2 Stylized Action for a Soloist

- The soprano singing the riddle scene in Act II of Puccini's *Turandot* is asked to deliver highly stylized movement language, with references to oriental theatre gesture. The costume is an elaborate robe, with wide sleeves, so she is provided with a rehearsal gown to work in.
- The movement needs a low stance, but she needs to be stable enough to sing the tricky passages, and to make the sustained posture and gestures resonant and meaningful.
- All explanation needs to be done quickly, simply and clearly, giving the soprano confidence and reassurance that she looks good and can feel secure in the physical material for the next rehearsal, which will be on stage.

Example 3 Acknowledging Vocal Demands

- In *Tristan and Isolde* Act III, Tristan sings a long aria. At this point in the story, he is dying, alone and weak, but the aria is powerful and impassioned.
- The challenge is to pay attention to making his waning strength visible and believable, while enabling him to sing the demanding passages.

He may be lying down and obviously needs to be comfortable, but with a sense of the pain and weakness he is experiencing.

- Crucially, he must be able to reach high notes, which are sung across heavy orchestration. He needs full lungs to deliver the music, and to be able to breathe deeply, accessing his full vocal support muscles. The diaphragm should not be twisted, and the singer can't use the strength in his legs to help support and boost the sound by being 'grounded'.
- This is a challenge for the singer and the movement director's knowledge of how the body is used in vocal production. It is also a paradox to overcome, in that strength required for vocal delivery may appear at odds with the believable physical weakness of the character at this point in the opera.

CONTEMPORARY OPERA PRODUCTION

Context

Regional opera companies in the USA and Europe, as contemporary ensembles, engage excellent singers, trained in music conservatoires, who have good acting ability and stage-craft skills, including movement, and are responsive to directorial instruction. Janis Kelly, international singer and vocal professor at the Royal College of Music, spoke to me about developments she participated in, led by opera director David Freeman. He founded the Opera Factory as an ensemble in London in 1981, which aimed to bring the theatre directing approaches of Peter Brook, and movement style akin to that of European approaches, to the staging of musical drama. This initiative was designed as a progressive development in contemporary staging through an immersive approach to acting and ensemble performance involving improvisation and movement skills for opera singers.

In contemporary opera productions, there is a sense of ensemble, with directors who expect improvisation, dramatic motivation and a range of working processes. Performers expect and benefit from movement guidance as they contribute to the creation of emerging work, in a way that may resemble contemporary theatre production. New and recently written contemporary operas can often be on a smaller scale than the repertoire of Baroque and nineteenth-century opera works and are often without a chorus.

Visual and Scenic Elements

The contemporary staging of opera is rich in visual elements and can involve epic scenic design on a large scale. An open stage, free of scenic elements, is unusual in opera. Issues arise with movement work and involve health and safety considerations if performers are asked to navigate a steeply raked stage, narrow balconies, unusual floor surfaces, staircases, flying elements or large pieces of hydraulically controlled moving scenic elements. The set, especially if it is a specially constructed unit with staircases and so on, will be in the rehearsal studio from day one. Beyond the hardware, powerful visual effects may be part of the design, created through digital means, such as video projection. These create superb effects, but prior knowledge of their inclusion is needed if interaction between movement and the technology is anticipated.

SINGING AND MOVEMENT

The instrument of the singer is not just the vocal cords but the whole body, and involves projecting the voice across the orchestra pit into the auditorium. Singers speak of their vocal support muscles, along with the need to feel 'grounded' for vocal delivery. As an instrument, the body is occupied in sound production and vocal technique, which involves training on a one-to-one basis with their teacher or coach. In contrast to how actors access expressive use of breath, breath control for a singer is integral to the timing and delivery of sung passages. Use of gesture and its timing in opera is also different from how an actor works. The singer needs to work with intention but respond also to the musical shape of a sung phrase, whereas the actor finds the rhythm of the action through intention, use of breath and the situation. Movement training and dance skills do not form a major part of the singers' training and skills vary considerably. Expectations within staging ideas by twenty-first-century directors mean that singers may be asked to perform material that is out of their physical comfort zone. The movement director needs to offer solutions that help the singer in rehearsal and navigate with them the demands of the stage production.

Emotion and the Body

The content of opera scenarios played out in arias and *recitative*, frequently moves through a full range of emotion. Expressing powerful, frequently negative, emotions (such as anger, sorrow, fear) can have a counter-productive effect on the body, in terms of creating additional tension or physical habits that are not always helpful in playing a character. Bodily awareness, relaxation, strength and stamina are needed to deliver embodied emotion but, ideally, not with the physical tension associated with real-life emotions.

Believable Characterization

Singing roles present a wide diversity of characters, who are expected to be believable, even if the role is of a person younger than the singer. The character may be human, requiring realistic believable portrayals, such as the sad and lonely Countess in the *Marriage of Figaro* (1786) or *Billy Budd* (1951) the sailor who is executed and *Peter Grimes* (1943) the lonely fisherman in Benjamin Britten's twentieth-century opera. Alternatively, the role may be a supernatural, mythic, heroic or alluring figure or deity. Examples include the ferocious and angry queen of the night in Mozart's *Magic Flute* (1791) or the water sprite in Dvorak's *Rusalka* (1901) and the gods and heroes of Wagner's *The Ring* (1876).

Movement Training for Singers

Singers who pursue advanced training and take up engagements in solo roles are chosen for their vocal potential and musicality. In the UK there are numerous schemes, such as the National Opera Studio and Young Artist schemes attached to the major companies, which offer extensive coaching in stagecraft and movement as an excellent grounding for the demands of a singing career. The major UK music conservatoires include movement training, which comprises movement coaching derived from a range of disciplines. This helps singers to increase body awareness, reduce tension and attend to alignment issues. There will also be a focus on experiences to awaken imaginative expression, movement awareness and using gesture and body language. Stage-craft equips the singer for the rehearsal process, stage presence, creation of a character and working with a director.

Movement Work in Opera Conservatoires

This includes:

- Increasing body awareness through regular exercises designed to sense and experience the body and its movement.
- Use of weight, flow, leg strength and alignment as carriage of the body.
- Examining expressive gesture as movement language and gaining confidence with its use.
- Dance forms encountered as music forms or set dances in an opera (waltz, minuet, polka).
- Working on physical characteristics for an aria or role.
- Preparing for auditions and recitals.
- Preparing 'trouser roles' for women who sing male roles (Cherubino in *Marriage of Figaro*, Octavian in *Der Rosenkavalier* and numerous Baroque opera roles).

The Box shows three simple tasks that are helpful for apprentice singers, with little or no stage experience, to become more aware and fluent with movement. Along with this could be exercises to feel 'grounded', to explore action in space and to understand the scale of movement and expression required in an aria or scene.

THE CHORUS

Almost all opera production involves a large chorus, although there are exceptions where there can be a small vocal ensemble or only soloists. A chorus in a large opera house can vary from thirty to eighty people, who are selected for their vocal skills and will have developed considerable stage experience.

MAINTAINING CONNECTION ACROSS THE SPACE IN A SCENE

Task 1 Maintaining Connection Across the Space

This exercise creates connections between performers and raises awareness of reading another person's movement. Ask two people to face each other and imagine that they are connected to each other by an invisible thread from a point on the chest, in the mid-sternum. The distance should be about two metres.

Ask them to relax their breathing, soften soles of the feet, their knees and hips joints, and imagine walking on a carpeted floor surface. Decide who is leading and following, and slowly ask each of them to go in the direction of the leader, who can choose forwards, sideways or back. Allow time to sense the significance of the weight shift involved in walking. The aim, eventually, is to not know who is leading or following but to be able to observe a soft sense of transition. This could be then tried with a sung passage, as a duet with improvised movement.

Task 2 A Journey to Cross the Stage Using Only Advance, Pause, Change Direction

This task is introduced to develop physical awareness and confidence for solo scene.

- Enter the space, moving along one line with the aim to arrive at the other side of the space, for example travel on the diagonal from one corner or laterally from stage left to stage right.
- Choose the starting point, speed, step length, direction of travel and arrival point.
- On the journey: make one stop, a change of direction, change of speed and continue.
- Once completed, choose a historical era and decide if the character is male or female.
- Invent or decide on the given circumstance of the moment, the place and environment.

Finally, link the journey to an aria or song being worked on and the circumstances of it. Try updating the story to contemporary times. For women working on a male role, explore the use of weight and physicality to find a gait, stance and convincing mode of walking for the character that avoids cliché.

Task 3 Express an Emotional State Using a Chair

This task aims to increase consciousness of the physicality of a character and what is being communicated.

- Where on the chair is your weight placed? Front edge of the seat? Leaning back?
- How are the legs placed in relation to it? Explore a range of actions, adding the arms.
- Explore one of six primary emotions: joy, sorrow, anger, disgust, fear, surprise.
- How can the rhythm of sitting, rising, collapsing and waiting be discovered in the aria?
- Explore how to give information by where the weight is placed, held or oriented.
- Repeat the task with a different use of weight, dynamics and bodily tension.

Observe the work of others doing this exercise and note what communicates well. Further:

- Use the chair and create a connection to it appropriate for a character or an aria.
- Explore different historical eras and contexts, including contemporary times.
- Examine how the physicality (for example) of sitting to drink in a pub in 1980s is different from a cocktail bar in 1950s New York.

Female chorus in *Carmen* directed by Sally Potter, ENO (2014).

It is likely that there will be a range of abilities in relation to movement and acting skills.

How is the Chorus Engaged?

A chorus member in a subsidized or state-funded company in Europe will be on a regular contract to sing for all productions in the repertoire. The chorus members will all know each other well, as they work closely together and, in the UK, tour together. With a regular chorus such as this, it is not usually appropriate to do company-building games with them. However, for opera festivals, such as Glyndebourne, singers are auditioned and engaged for just that season. They may not all know one another well, nor have worked together before. It can be beneficial to offer movement work and improvisation tasks as part of a creative approach to devising material, providing its purpose for the production is understood and explained.

Workload and Repertoire

An opera chorus in the UK, USA and Europe is professional, willing to try new things, both in staging and movement, and is extremely hard-working. It is worth having respect for what the chorus singer's workload entails. In any one week a chorus could be doing all of these:

- Learning the music for a new opera or a revival, not yet in studio rehearsal.
- Rehearsing the staging of a different opera, in the studio, as a new production or revival.
- Attending stage and piano or orchestra rehearsals in costume.
- Performing the current repertoire each night in one of up to three different operas.

Handling Large Groups

When dealing with this large body of experienced professionals, the movement director needs a cool head and an ability to offer clear, relevant and non-wavering instructions to the singers. Rehearsal time with the chorus is not normally extensive and it is worth making an enquiry about the total number of sessions and stage calls they will attend. It is important to balance the rehearsal of the opera staging by planning with the director on how to include physical warm-ups and making time for taught material with new or challenging dance skills as part of the rehearsal process. There will be no other time to do it. It is important to realize that older and experienced chorus members may have worked on at least three previous revivals of a well-known, often performed work being prepared. They are very likely to have an opinion about what is new to them and will tell you all about that.

Clarity

It is vital to create material and action with the chorus in a way that enables them, as performers, to be engaged in the story of what they are singing. It is worth taking time to explain, briefly and clearly, the reasons behind any movement material being developed. Any chorus also needs to be able to deliver the music and any vocal demands comfortably, whilst moving and offering the appropriate dramatic, emotional intentions being requested by the director. Knowledge of the score and libretto is the best ally for this; as is learning key words or phrase from the lyrics. Ways need to be found to help with the development of ideas and managing large numbers.

Working Strategies

Large chorus scenes can be challenging, and a strategy needs to be developed to handle large numbers and to keep everyone engaged and working creatively. Phyllida Lloyd on several productions used a strategy to break down the hierarchy and distance between the soloists and the large chorus that is usual in opera. She used an approach that helped the outcomes of the production and served the narrative in which a smaller group of twelve singers was selected from different vocal groups. Material created with them was then shared to involve the entire chorus. This approach was used for *Gloriana* at Opera North in 1996, for the staging of Verdi's *Requiem* at ENO in 2002 and *Carmelites* in 2005. With Britten's *Peter Grimes* at Opera North in 2006, an 'inner chorus' was established who played members of the 'Borough' and were on an equal status with the soloists, who played the vicar, the schoolteacher, a retired seaman, the pub landlady and fishermen of the village community. The creation of a believable community meant that material, identities, motivation and action were shared as an ensemble, as if working on a play.

Planning and Time Management

Nothing quite prepares the movement director or the director for their first full chorus call. Even confident and experienced theatre directors turn to jelly at the daunting prospect of the numbers involved. It pays huge dividends to acquire, in advance, a full set of photos of the chorus members, in their vocal groups and to learn their names. It is a good strategy to

Peter Grimes. Jefferey Lloyd Roberts, with Roderick Williams, Christopher Purves and the chorus of Opera North (2006).

explain simply when something abstract in terms of movement is required, or if a moment of acting realism is required. If the movement and action aim to avoid a staging or acting cliché, explain helpfully and clearly what is required and trust the experience of the group. Experience in terms of the chorus comes in many guises, so it pays off to establish your style and taste, and to offer some helpful techniques toward achieving this will reap rewards. Good memories and great moments emerge when an experienced, helpful, hard-working chorus all buy into the process of what is needed. Guidance is all, as is taking the chorus seriously for their expertise and experience, which avoids the emergence of unhelpful group behaviour, which can undermine confidence in the material being developed, and the preparation and process of the creative team.

Chorus Availability

It is advisable to discuss the advance schedule of the chorus in a meeting well ahead of the first rehearsals and to make clear the needs for the production. As the production takes shape, it is likely that more rehearsal time may need to be negotiated with the opera company management. In opera companies, two and sometimes three productions will be in rehearsal simultaneously, and the chorus will only be

AT A PRELIMINARY MEETING...

The opera had seven to eight complex scenes or *tableaux* of vivid stage action for a chorus of around sixty people. The director, new to opera, but with a rich and imaginative vision for the staging needed guidance on the planning of the time. On checking the advance schedule, it was discovered that only five sessions of three hours had been allocated for all of the chorus scenes. Clearly this presented an impossible scenario. In the ensuing production meeting with the management, brisk words were exchanged. A firm request to double that number and add two additional sessions was made, to achieve the extensive movement and staging work for the production. The wish was granted but not without taking some sessions away from the music department, who were outraged. It was not a peaceful creation period but a highly successful production.

Mephistopheles and the chorus, *La Damnation de Faust*, Théâtre du Châtelet, Paris (1990).

able to come to specific sessions. In truth, in a repertoire company the chorus will be actively involved for the season, in rehearsing, preparing and performing about five operas at a time. It pays to respect the demands made on these hard-working musicians and what they carry in terms of music knowledge, text and staged action. Rehearsal sessions are three hours long, with a twenty-minute break, which must be observed. There are Musicians' Union rules (to which choristers belong) about the number of sessions per week and the chorus members being given time for costume fittings and to get into and out of costumes during stage rehearsals and performances.

Rehearsal Schedules

In planning for the movement direction of a series of large chorus scenes, the first questions to be ascertained are:

- How many full chorus scenes are required for the libretto and score?

- How many sessions have been allocated by the company?
- Is dance material involved?
- Are the principal singers involved in any scenes?
- Will the whole chorus be available at all the stage rehearsals?
- Does the director want to use the chorus for scenes or staging in additional to sung scenes?

NON-SINGING PERFORMERS

Actors or Supers

This group of performers is, of course silent and can also be called *figurants* (a French term meaning figures), supernumerary performers or 'supers', simply 'extras', and in UK productions are called actors. These performers provide a range of characters, notably servants and can also enable scene changes of onstage set elements. More recently, specific sequences of material and action for the overture of an opera have been created with actors. A good example is David McVicar's Royal Opera production of *Marriage of Figaro*, where the servants feature in a staged sequence for the overture. Large opera houses have regular employees experienced in a range of movement styles and can be familiar with the operatic works and also directorial styles within the repertoire. Any new production ideally requires that performers are auditioned for their movement training and skills, with evidence of their experience of music when hiring. These performers can function as a movement group with multiple roles or with a particular movement style throughout the production. It is worth sharing with the director the views you have on the skills required and that you might want to draw out in creating with these performers.

Dancers

Dancers are usually engaged for featured choreography (ballet music written into an opera, for example) and to dance in aspects of the staging beyond the skill of actor/movers. With their specialist training, it is important to have an allocated studio and a dance captain, or assistant, from within the group to offer a formal class or warm-up for all dancers throughout rehearsals and performances. If hired for a season of opera, dancers may be required to appear in a couple of different operas and it is worth checking with forward-planning how much time is assigned to each production. Worth avoiding is a situation in which dancers are kept waiting around during a long rehearsal, often in a crowded room with little space for offstage practice and then be expected to jump up and perform a scene full out. Dancers do need to be prepared to mix and mingle with non-dancers, with the chorus, as well as appearing in featured moments. They also need to be discouraged from elaborate stretching routines or practising impressive tricks during rehearsals, which can be distracting.

Specialist Performers

Contemporary opera production values mean that physical theatre, martial arts, puppetry, bungee wire skills, stilt walkers and/or acrobatic elements may be required. The visual aspect of opera performance is increasingly used to powerful effect and will require specific technical expertise. These diverse skill backgrounds and training may be beyond the skills of the movement director, and it is important to discuss carefully with the director and designer

Dancers in a stage rehearsal of *Turandot*, Madrid (2008).

ways to integrate this specialist material into the world of the production. If the performers' skill is not one you are familiar with, it is wise to respect their knowledge and discuss their needs ahead of rehearsals if possible. It is worth finding out:

- If further use of the specialist performers in other roles will be required within the staging.
- If the performers will rehearse 'off-site' and how warm-up and travel time are calculated.
- What these specialist performers require (equipment and so on) to do their work safely.
- Who prepares the risk assessment and has a duty of care for its implementation?

Working with Children

It is a huge pleasure to work with children in the opera context. New productions include children as singers and actors to accentuate dramaturgical points in the staging. Children provide not only innocence, vulnerability or sense of play, but also offer a contrast to darker, grander and more powerful ideas. Working with children requires considered, professional attitudes, which can mean respect for each young individual, along with kindness, encouragement and reassurance, in what may be an unfamiliar territory to them.

Examples of Children's Roles

In Mozart's *Magic Flute* there are three boys whose recurring sung role contributes memorably to the story. Benjamin Britten's *Peter Grimes* has a role for the boy apprentice whom Grimes is accused of killing, who also appears as a ghost.

Boris Godunov in Andrei Tarkovsky's iconic 1983 production at Royal Opera, Covent Garden, had a memorable enigmatic role played by a small, blonde-haired boy, whose recurring appearance connected with the tolling of a bell and time passing.

Benjamin Britten's *Gloriana* (1994) at Opera North in Leeds, directed by Phyllida Lloyd, had a group of twelve small boys who sang and danced as the Country Maidens in the Norwich Masque scene. It was common practice in Elizabethan theatre and masques for boy actors to play girls. The local

Leeds schoolboys needed some persuading to wear the dresses and flowered coronets required. However, Phyllida Lloyd kindly offered the concession that they could wear their breeches and boots as well to show they were dressing for the part as young actors.

Child-Protection Issues

Child-protection rules issued are regularly updated by the government and need to be understood and respected in line with the opera company policy whenever children under eighteen attend rehearsals and perform in an opera production. It is not permitted to work alone in a studio with children under the age of eighteen, without an official Disclosure and Barring Service (DBS) certificate, or without supervision by someone holding a DBS certificate. Whenever children, either as choristers, in solo roles or as extras, are engaged to work within an opera production, a chaperone or two will be required to be present in all rehearsals that the movement director might lead. Their job is to manage and care for the children when not rehearsing any acting, dancing or movement. Children generally rehearse out of school hours, and break times for them may vary from the professional company ones. Special arrangements can be made for children in specific roles to attend rehearsals during the day, stage rehearsals and a full company run through.

Working with children.

RESEARCH

Organizing and undertaking movement research for historical accuracy, and to recreate for atmosphere, style and context in opera, are very valuable when creating the movement language as a believable reality. For example, *The Rake's Progress* opera by Stravinsky could need information gleaned from William Hogarth's paintings regarding social etiquette at public events attended by the aspiring Tom Rakewell. Along with this, references for understanding of the physicality of a lunatic asylum of the eighteenth century, and the potential to depict it through the bodies of the actors. Research would enable accurate work with the lead character to portray his rise in society followed by his desperate decline. Hogarth's paintings give an accurate and detailed portrait of the story set in that time. However, the director might decide to set the opera in the decadence of 1970s New York, which would need a very different set of references and research.

Movement Director Kate Flatt – *The Carmelites* by Francis Poulenc (1957), Directed by Phyllida Lloyd, English National Opera (2005)

Poulenc's *The Dialogue of the Carmelites* is set in a Carmelite convent in Compiègne in France and tells of a real event, the martyrdom of fifteen nuns, following the French revolution. During the reign of terror, those in religious orders were banned from holding mass and these nuns, rather than renounce their faith, were imprisoned and then condemned to death by guillotine. The opera ends with an epic version of the *Salve Regina*, as the fifteen nuns go one by one to their death. The revival of *The Carmelites* at ENO and WNO in 1999 and 2006 created a Carmelite community, with soloists and chorus, and the crucial focus was on the identity of each nun as the story unfolds.

Background Research

We were curious about the physical world and ritual of the religious and devotional life of the Carmelites. I made contact by letter with the Mother Prioress at the enclosed, silent order of the Carmelites, at their convent in Notting Hill and secured a meeting

with her. When I arrived, I waited in anteroom, then was shown into a room with a curtained grille. The Mother Prioress drew back a curtain and we faced each other from either side of the grille. We discussed the clothing, the habit, veil and other garments, as well as the movement language used by the nuns and how they communicate with each other following the vow of silence. There are codes of movement and sign language within their formal, silent world that hark back centuries. The Mother Prioress I met became a nun before the reforms of the second Vatican Council in 1965. She was able to show me the formal greeting for a superior (kneeling and being blessed) and spoke of how daily offices or services were conducted. She allowed me also to watch the nuns from the public part of the chapel, through the grille, with the curtain open again, and the formal language of their departure after mass. It was stimulating to have this (literal) window into a completely different world. The research as information given by a practising nun from inside a closed order gave detailed insights drawn from a source that has stayed unbroken as a tradition.

Process

Movement work drew on this research and contributed by establishing the convent world as a believable yet entirely other reality in terms of behaviour, with the brown habits of the nuns starkly outlined within the white walls of the set by Anthony Ward. As a part of the rehearsal process, the ritual of 'profession', in which a novice lies down with arms outstretched, was re-enacted. She was covered with cloths as a 'burial', which signifies the death of her old life and taking up the new as a nun. The details of the habit and its importance to communication and the body were very important. The hierarchy of the silent order of Carmelites was examined, their devotion to prayer and the cycle of the day and the offices. At the end, as the fifteen martyrs sing the *Salve Regina*, each nun was seen to make the decision to go to her death by guillotine, with the whine of the blade audibly falling, but the death not visible.

GENERATING MATERIAL IN REHEARSAL

Peter Grimes (1945) by Benjamin Britten, Directed by Phyllida Lloyd, Opera North (2006)

The chorus scenes in *Peter Grimes* require staging and movement material that capture the groundswell of emotional shifts and collective judgement of Peter Grimes, a loner and fisherman, deemed a villain by the tight-knit community of a fishing village, known as 'the Borough'. To achieve a physicality that resembled a working, fishing community, the chorus were asked to take part in an exercise of hauling ropes as if landing a boat. With this energy of muscular memory in their bodies, a portrayal of unified, work activity was created as a grounded, wide stance, sustained sway, with weight shifting powerfully from side to side. The opening and closing scenes of the opera involved a giant suspended fishing net, almost the diameter of the stage, flooded with white light by Paule Constable's lighting design. The entire chorus and cast were spaced around the outstretched, circular net, holding the edges of it, with a smaller group of women in the centre, as if repairing it. No musical counts were given for this unsung passage of Britten's music, and the singers synchronized with one another, unified by the tempo from the music. It was as if the movement of the sea was making them sway. There was a return to this powerful image at the end of the opera. When the music came to an end, they continued to sway, moving in rhythm, with just the creaking of oil skins in the palpable silence, as the lights faded at the end of the opera.

Betrothal in a Monastery (1946) by Prokoviev, Directed by Daniel Slater, Glyndebourne Festival (2006)

For the monks' chorus in Act II, the set by Robert Innes Hopkins was a large pit, lined with skulls, with a huge, hinged cover that was raised to reveal the activity, and lowered at the end of the scene on the ensuing riotous action. To achieve the tone and style, images from artists Hieronymus Bosch and Francisco Goya were used. These offered graphic imagery of grotesque figures and many ideas for licentious, and somewhat bawdy, action. There

Peter Grimes, opening and closing sequence.

were approximately twenty-four singers playing the monks, plus three physical theatre performers with specialist dance and acrobatic skills mixed in with the chorus. They were asked to form groups of three to four and engage in a task to generate material. Their choices from this were used, giving vibrant, layered detail to the ensemble action for the scene. The following task was given to the chorus and proved a viable way of creating a group response, which captured mood and intent drawn from the images. As a task it was useful to ask them to:

- Recreate the moment of the image and then imagine what could precede and follow it.
- Imagine the physicality of the characters depicted.
- Explore their gait and placing of their weight.
- Imagine what speed might they move at.

MOVEMENT AND DANCE IN OPERA

The use of social and historical dance in opera is an important area to address. Dance written into operas, as diegetic dance, is related to the specific music for which it is intended. The dance is referred to in the libretto, and in which the characters participate in the dances as social interaction. A movement director arranges a dance and develops the material from the reasons revealed in the story and the director's vision as to why the dance is happening and its purpose within the opera. There is an important distinction between dance sequences as choreography and dance in a context where performers are interacting in a realistic manner – not in formally arranged choreography – this is diegetic dance.

Tchaikovsky's *Eugene Onegin* has a peasant dance in Act I, a waltz and cotillion in mazurka rhythm in Act II and the polonaise and ecossaise in Act III. The musical indications are very specific. All but the Ecossaise and peasant dance are in different types of 3/4 rhythm with different accents stressed in the dance steps. The dances will most likely be performed by the chorus and principal singers with dancers in addition. A director may decide to ask instead for a sequence, timed to the dance music of the score, as a concept that provides a commentary on the action. In terms of style, dances in opera range from social dance, ballet, contemporary dance to folk dance. Contemporary staging of older operas or newly composed works show increasing diversity of dance forms referenced within them. For example, Rameau's Baroque opera ballet *Les Indes Galantes* (1736) was given a contemporary staging at the Paris Opera in 2017, which used hip-hop choreography by Bintou Dembélé, with dancers and accompanying movement for the chorus to excellent effect.

The Gospel According to the Other Mary (2012) by John Adams, Directed by Peter Sellars, ENO (2014)

Ingrid Mackinnon recalls that one of the artists that Peter Sellars brought over for the London production was a New York krump artist, Banks, who played the Angel Gabriel. Both buck and krump dance forms are unusual to find in contemporary opera. As a 'buck' dancer he had solo material throughout the entire work, which was in direct contrast to the movement language of the chorus. They offered the vocal percussion with the score and with gesture as is common in Sellars' work. Banks was offering physical percussion through his use of the dance form and embodiment of that material in relation to the music. It was clear that he heard the music his own way. It was so magical to watch, and I think there were many chorus members who were distracted because they just couldn't take their eyes off him. Meanwhile, in contrast, I was on stage playing Mary Magdalene and moving very slowly. Peter Sellars kept telling me to move slower and slower, even though I wanted to be up there doing the buck dancing!

The Bartered Bride (1866) by Smetana, Directed by Rudolf Nolte, Welsh National Opera (1983)

The scene involved a group of villagers dancing a polka, in a large barn. The emphasis of the production was on realism and sustained emotional truth in the storytelling. The brief from the rather grumpy director was 'peasant dancing cannot be interesting for more than 45 seconds – we will have to cut the music...'.

Time was allocated (unusually an hour and a half per day for a whole week) for the forty chorus members to learn dances for specific music. At traditional village dances in Slovakia and Transylvania, the couples improvise through a range of figures, without set material as such. With the chorus, each couple learned a series of four- and eight-bar figures. Rather than set steps or patterns, each couple chose the figures, which they danced within the musical framework, in their own way and as if for their own pleasure. The director returned to watch the work and asked, 'How did you do this? The mood is perfect'. The music did not need to be cut. The material was lightly structured to enable clarity in repetition for every performance. Some couples were featured and placed downstage and an old man, an extra performer, danced with three small children. A collective enjoyment and vitality were created so that the audience felt their mood. It produces a different look from the order of shaped choreographic patterns.

Marriage of Figaro (1786) by Mozart, Directed by John Cox, Garsington Opera (2005)

The fandango in *Marriage of Figaro* is during Susanna and Figaro's wedding as part of the nuptials. There is sung dialogue integral to the plot, which takes place during the dance, and the singers need to be downstage front and the detail of passing a note to be visible for the audience. Despite a lot of searching, the actual steps of the fandango were somewhat elusive. Casanova is recorded as saying it is 'the most lascivious of dances' (Curt Sachs, *World History of the Dance*). However the pair dances, the *sevillanas* (from Seville, as its name implies, where the opera is set) offers an appropriate match with the fandango, as it is a dance of attraction where the couple circle each other seductively, and end with close embrace. Mozart's music for the fandango is written as a minuet and has a relatively sedate charm. The *sevillanas* is in 6/8 time, whereas the minuet is in 3/4 time, but the way the accents fall in the bar creates an interesting juxtaposition. The minuet, if counted across two bars, has accents on second and sixth beats 123 and 456 and the *sevillanas* is accented on the first and fourth beats 123 456. With added patterning of the group, hip swaying, lowered centre of gravity, beaten or stamped accents, with the interaction of the couples, a sense of celebration was created for the fandango.

Don Giovanni (1787), Directed by John Caird, Welsh National Opera (2011)

In the trio sung by Don Ottavio, Donna Anna and Donna Elvira, preceding the minuet and party scene in Act II, the plan was for the whole chorus to come on stage, one by one, very slowly at the start of the scene. They were asked to soften their knees as they walked, confidently and smoothly, feeling drawn to the centre of the space, but without making a sound. It was explained to the chorus that it was to give a semblance of a dance, in a dreamlike way, as in

Greek by Mark Anthony Turnage. Working with frieze images.

gathering and wanting to dance. The unfolding slow motion needed the imagined grace and etiquette of an earlier age – that of the time of the opera in seventeenth-century Spain. The stage was divided into three zones with the chorus forming three circles – one in each zone. Each circle of people did a suggestion of an old dance using a light, elegant 'hands right and left' action from a contredanse, but very slowly, passing one another in a chain-like fashion, and making connection across the space.

Over their long dresses, the women wore silk chiffon, wing-like shawls, which draped along their arms. In their midst, Don Giovanni arrived and like moths to a flame, the women were drawn to him, forming one large circular throng with him at the centre lifting their arms, so the light caught the opaque silk shawls. Then the slow music changed abruptly to a rapid galop, and a hectic party ensued. What was important, and worked successfully, was that there did not need to be too much information or instruction to take on board. The three key indications were:

- The physicality and style required for all.
- The arrival point of the image to be achieved and the musical cue.
- The musical cues to listen for in terms of change of action.

CASE STUDY OF CONTEMPORARY OPERA STAGING

Movement Director Jenny Ogilvie – *Greek* (1988) by Mark-Anthony Turnage, Directed by Joe Hill-Gibbins, Scottish Opera (2018)

The opera *Greek* from Steven Berkoff's 1980s play, with music by Mark-Anthony Turnage, tells the story of Sophocles' *Oedipus Rex* but set in the East End of London of Thatcher's Britain. Both score and libretto are incredibly playful and shapeshift their way from the grotesque to the absolute sublime via music hall, football chants, punk provocation and megaphones of riot police. There is a small cast of four singers with Eddy (Oedipus) as the main singer, and all the other parts played by a further three singers. These characters essentially embody the archetypes of 'Mum', 'Dad' and 'Wife'.

The Design

The set design, by Johannes Schütz, referenced the setting of an ancient Greek tragedy, while the costumes, by Alex Lowde, were a brilliant contemporary take on aspirational 1980s Britain. The playing space was very shallow, comprising a high platform, backed by a huge white wall that filled the entire proscenium, with two doorways, one on each side,

Body work with the singers.

Finding the punk body.

cut into it. Arranged like this, the playing space was a gift in several ways:

- The platform was situated as far forward of the proscenium arch as it could be, which meant that the singers could really take advantage of being pushed so close to the audience that they were able to confront or confide in them.
- The platform was also very high and seemed to have no 'way off', creating literally no escape for Eddy, who stayed on the platform almost throughout.
- There were two doorways cut into the wall, one on each side, which meant that we could bring the three singers on through one door and off via the other, in a bewildering cycle of variations. This way, Eddy was confronted by the same archetypes each time a set of 'new' characters entered.
- Finally, at several key moments, the whole wall turned on its central axis point, swinging out over the audience. This was an incredible piece of stage design. I couldn't believe it was happening every time I saw it and felt it communicating the machinations of fate in a visceral way.

Physical Language

Director Joe Hill-Gibbins and I had an absolute ball finding references for the piece and it helped that we could both draw on the mutual experience of our childhood in 1980s Britain. Our references ranged from the credit sequence of TV series *Howard's Way*, the Sex Pistols in live performances, classi-

cal ballet (Eddy even did a beautiful *assemblé* leap in the Love Duet), school textbook graffiti, smutty seaside postcards, Action Man and the Girl's World headspace, and Derek Jarman's iconic film *Jubilee* (1978). Whilst much of the fun of the piece lay in pushing our use of these references to the maximum, it was also very important to have a strong and cohesive physical performance style to provide a consistent framework for all the *fantasie*.

The Creative Process

We devised a set of physical rules for the piece and really pushed the singers to embody them fully as we knew it was vital to the success of the piece. In devising these principles, I looked at ancient Greek friezes to see what devices those artists used to make the storytelling dynamic in two dimensions. Then I turned these into a set of physical rules for the company, which helped the singers amplify and clarify their physical storytelling. It also made it clear to the audience that we had chosen a heightened playing style that was specific to the world of the opera.

Devices and rules for developing the physicality were defined as follows:

- Gaze – a hyper-animated connection with the audience, which was specific to the main character, who addressed the audience directly throughout. We studied the physicality of punk performers like Johnny Rotten to understand how he could find the maximum engagement with the audience by playfully shocking, provoking and teasing them.

- Glue – consciously moulding in close proximity, as a couple or group, and then keeping this connection 'hummingly' alive when distanced or as the couple or group move apart.
- Shape and stretch – when the singers found bold, physical shapes, we encouraged them to stretch them by 10 per cent extra, making the material clearly legible as a two-dimensional statement.
- Grow and twist – growing into (and radiating beyond) a bold physical shape then twisting it to a new shape. We used this to create a variety of group shapes that radiated wider but still had 'bound' energy.
- Three against one – consciously playing the space with an awareness of the various group dynamics to be found when a group of three is pitched against one.
- Stops and starts – being very specific about when and where a journey started and stopped. Footwork and orientation of the body was incredibly exposed by the playing space, which meant that the performers had to be either facing out or in profile and take no unnecessary steps.
- Doorways – the doorways were such a powerful element of the set, and it was important that the singers were very specific about positions held in doorways or the way they entered through them.

The Punk Body

We defined the key characteristic of the physicality as the 'punk body'. This was used to explore the style and acknowledged, or used, all the following approaches in working toward the result:

- Childlike release of energy.
- Use of floor, and off-centre of gravity.
- Unapologetic body.
- Direct (aggressive/playful) opposition to audience.
- Wide-eyed (outrage/hostility).
- Released/draped arms (ape-like).
- Posing in distorted/exaggerated shapes.
- To impress, challenge, seduce, offend.

Greek stage set in rehearsal.

CHAPTER 8

MOVEMENT DIRECTION APPLIED IN OTHER CONTEXTS

The main areas of live theatre-making where movement directors practise their craft are covered in Chapters 6 and 7. However, introduced here are examples of the wider application of movement direction skills, which indicate career development for diverse areas. These include the specialist skills and artistry in emerging fields, which are changing and growing with technology, or other skills and their interface with movement direction. Physical comedy relates to the timeless and significant theatre practice of clowning and mime, and is a specialist field. Intimacy coordination is an emerging field, and very much in the *Zeitgeist* in how it embraces safe practice and respect for performers working with intimate engagement. New technology is the driver behind motion capture, as is virtual reality, in film and TV. The different movement direction roles introduced here are in appreciation of the diverse impact that the craft and skill of movement practitioners is making in the development of the following areas:

- Film and TV.
- Contemporary circus.
- Motion capture.
- Intimacy co-ordination.
- Fashion shoots and promotions.
- Physical comedy.

FILM

Movement direction in film encompasses a big field, well beyond the scope of this book, with movement practitioners who have migrated from live theatre or dance to work for the camera. Movement work on a film can take place over an extended period of several weeks during a studio shoot or on location. The work is wide-ranging and multiple levels of expertise may be called upon that involve supervision of a 'department' with responsibility for locating and recruiting either a group of performers or solo movement artists or dancers as a 'stand-in' for a star throughout a film shoot. The movement work itself could be to create historical accuracy in a costume drama of a particular era, which will need to be researched and developed in tandem with a composer or music arranger. More futuristic work could include the development of a physicality as behavioural language for large groups of performers – often called movement artists – playing aliens, zombies or mythical creatures. Highly specialized work beyond the movement director's skill is done by martial arts and fight experts, involving film technology for non-realistic illusion such as in Ang Lee's *Crouching Tiger Hidden Dragon* (2000). A movement director's work can include the design and styling of a leading role with detailed creation of a physicality for one or two performers, such as

OPPOSITE: **The physical humour of performer Jos Houben.**

Toby Sedgewick's carefully observed and detailed recreation of Laurel and Hardy's work, played by Steve Coogan and John C. Reilly in *Stan and Ollie* (2017). On set, coaching by a movement director for one performer is generally called cast support. Movement director Polly Bennet worked with actor Rami Malek as Freddie Mercury in *Bohemian Rhapsody* (2018) and Alexandra Reynolds worked with Eddie Redmayne as Stephen Hawking in *The Theory of Everything* (2014) and *The Danish Girl* (2015).

CONTEMPORARY CIRCUS AND MOVEMENT DIRECTION

Vicki Amedume, Artistic Director of Upswing, in conversation (2021)

Contemporary circus, acrobatic and aerial work involves action that is outside the realm of what normal bodies do on a day-to-day basis. Circus involves non-pedestrian movement and creates big moments, but it can also create small, delicate moments. In performance it can articulate something about the human condition and relationships with other people or to other spaces.

Background

I come from a contemporary circus background and my training was as a circus practitioner. Circus communicates through skills, and circus training develops both skills and strength in practice. I trained in the UK and in France, spending six months at Centre National des Arts du Cirque in Châlons-en-Champagne. The centre offers a range of approaches, such as working with music, movement, dance and theatrical practice, thinking about skills as a form of articulation rather than a practice in themselves.

Circus and Movement

My interest as a maker is driven thematically and starts from an idea, then goes on to thinking how I can articulate this physically, often without text. Movement direction has always informed what I do, because there has never been a point where I've made work that was only about a demonstration of

skill. I've always been interested in speaking to an idea or a theme. In my strategies around creating with circus bodies, I've realized that I work more with movement direction than pure circus technique.

I have always associated movement direction with text-based theatre. In the past when I have been brought in to the production of a play, to work on circus and aerial elements, I've been asked to be a 'circus consultant' or a 'technical consultant' as there may already be a movement director working across the whole piece. However, I find there is often a need for me to translate into action what a director is imagining as an idea, or a moment that incorporates and can communicate through circus. In my practice, I get excited about taking on an idea and the motivation behind it, so that what develops in a scene drives the action. My work is to translate that into something physical using the skills I have, which are primarily circus – aerial and acrobatics.

Circus and Narrative

When I'm developing a concept or reading a script, either for my own work or with another director, I'm looking for opportunities for circus to crystallize an idea or move something forwards as communication with the audience. If it's a linear narrative, it will mean working from the script and figuring out how circus can be incorporated to move the scene forwards. It is a real process of translation and working from what is underpinning a moment or dynamic. It then offers an anchor in the idea or the emotion, and becomes something that audiences will recognize. This can be compared to musical theatre, and how there is that moment where the dialogue stops and the song begins, and as if nothing more can be said, something new is revealed to you, or you are being taken on a journey with the character. Circus in a linear narrative often functions in that same way.

Upswing

Upswing is a leading contemporary circus company, 'whose productions and creative engagement programmes use circus to unite people from different backgrounds, uncover the extraordinary potential in humans and explore the ideas and stories that can

Teaching circus skills at Upswing.

connect us as communities' (https://upswing.org.uk, August 2021).

Upswing was formed in response to several things. As a black practitioner in a mainly white, Eurocentric art form, I wanted to create a space to discover my creative voice and what it was to be authentic to myself, and the practice that fully embraced my body and identity. As a performer, working mainly on other people's shows, I began to have opinions about what I would like to be doing! That's the time to start making your own work. I have been working under the name Upswing since 2002 and once we received more substantial funding in 2012, we were able to formalize the organization. Circus is an individualized art form and I am often looking for very specific skills for different pieces of work. This can make it difficult to work with the same group of performers over time, unless we were able to afford an ensemble of nine to twelve performers to work with as a regular ensemble. With the company, the shows now tend to have a long life, so we can develop something with one collective and know that we will work with them (however sporadically) for a while.

Training Offered

At Upswing, I give artistic and dramaturgical training to other circus practitioners, helping them to think about how they bring meaning to what they are creating. Contemporary circus within the performing arts industry is becoming more professionalized and expensive to enter. One of Upswing's aims is to offer entry routes into the industry for talented folk with no formal circus training, particularly global majority artists.

MOTION CAPTURE

This is a specialist field that engages with technology used to capture human movement as digital data. It is a growing field, with the demand for new themes and characters to be created in animated form for TV, film, theatre, live performance and the lucrative industry of video games. The work of the movement director is embedded in the process of production involved in creating a video game. In production, there are different departments for specific areas, with teams of creative practitioners, who work on the same scene or scenario, but probably don't even meet.

Asha Jennings-Grant – Movement Director and Motion Capture Practitioner
Context

I am currently working for an audio production company that provides the character performances

Motion capture performer with digital image.

that are part of the video games using motion capture technology. I create qualities of movement with multi-skilled performers. For example, if there is a race of creatures (such as giants, goblins or ogres), I work together with the group of performers to create the physicality so that everyone involved in the action clearly understands the way they should move – as in style, speed, physical characteristics and so forth. The clients developing the video game, who create and commission the concept or scenario, watch the emerging work on a monitor, remotely. From time to time, they will send through notes to the studio in response to what they observe and like or would prefer to be developed differently. These responses will mean that new action must be generated or existing material has to be adapted. This means that the movement work is continually changing and being revised.

Teamwork

It is teamwork. I can often begin an idea that is later progressed by someone else, or I can find myself developing and continuing the shaping of work begun by someone else. Our job title is

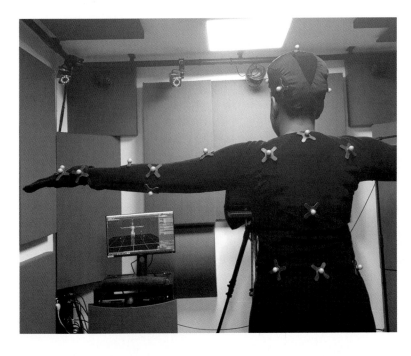

Performer in a motion capture suit.

'performance director' and we rarely meet others in the team, but we share the working process as the emerging work moves forward. There is no sense of single ownership or authorship in this open, creative environment, whereby several different movement practitioners create the work.

Physical Language

As a brief, I am given a description of a character, who might be an imagined mythical being. I am given the age or size and told that he might be armed or have other unusual characteristics, such as being very upright, for example. He could also have personality traits and be described as arrogant, a bit strange or only appear at night. Further description may give a clue about the physicality required for a character or group of characters and might include brief information on the dynamics of a character's movement, for example relaxed, having predatory grace, twitchy, grounded or weighty. Actual movement or description of the action is not usually given, allowing myself as movement or performance director to create and devise the action with the performer.

Creating a Physicality to Match a Voice

The company I work for provides audio dialogue and voices for the characters in the game. My role is described by the clients as 'performance director' and serves to support the voice director who is also creating the character in the working sessions. We work together to establish a physical character, whereby I design the movement to match the voice through a collaborative process involving the voice director, myself and the performer actually doing the movement.

Limitations and Challenges

Unusually, I am not in the same space as the performer. I give instructions from a sound-proofed booth using a microphone, which can be a challenge, being unable to demonstrate the movement. Most of the time, I don't have any actual contact with the performer, nor can they see me, as they are in a separate room on the other side of a glass window. I need to work quite fast with motion capture to

achieve a result that also reads well. The desired aim is to create a believable portrayal (even if a fictional character) as a well-rounded performance for the shoot. What I co-create will become part of the final video game after considerable further work by a post-production team.

INTIMACY CO-ORDINATION

On film and TV productions, opera and theatre contexts intimacy coordination is movement work for scenes with sexual content. In *Actor Movement* by Vanessa Ewan and Debbie Green (2015), chapter 4, pp. 247–250, there is a clear comparison made between intimacy work and that of the fight director in stage combat. In a fight sequence, violence and combat manoeuvres are developed technically as a series of actions, to be convincing and yet wholly safe for the performers. A fight scene takes into consideration the character's dramatic through-line for a scene. Similarly, intimate or sexual scenes are part of the characters' behaviour and closely related to their character as portrayed within the play or film. Movement work involving intimacy is structured in a way that enables the actors to navigate the scene and engage with authenticity of intentions, which may be entirely without dialogue but involve breathing and vocalized responses.

Ita O'Brien, Intimacy Co-ordinator, in conversation (2020)

Ita O'Brien is a movement director who specializes in work on scenes of an intimate nature, which take place in films, TV and theatre. Recent TV productions have drawn attention to the role and how the support is given to performers in preparation and shooting of these scenes. The approach of an intimacy co-ordinator in terms of content, character and action indicates respect for the actors. Ita runs courses in intimacy coordination, which serve to extend the role of the movement director into this field. The very nature of working on a closed set, however, precludes any possibility to observe the work undertaken, as only those involved in shooting the scene are allowed to be present.

Code of Practice

Intimacy coordination acknowledges the physical and emotional journey the actor may have to make in rehearsing and shooting scenes with sensitive material. The aim is to lead actors away from the 'personal body' and any reference to real life, by concentrating on clarity of action and the 'beats' for a sequence of moves. The approach avoids the possibility of performers feeling exposed or exploited by any gratuitous use of sex or nudity in a scene. Intentions in a script may touch on highly sensitive areas such as sexual violence or rape and connect with past traumatic personal stories. If the scene involves sexual violence, there needs to be awareness of disturbing triggers within the memory of a performer. This will lead to discussions of limitations and boundaries for the actor about what is permissible and what is off-limits for the scene. Intimacy on Set, Code of Conduct Guidelines have been established in the UK and are like those already in use in the USA. They outline what is appropriate while rehearsing and shooting a film, play or opera, and what is not. The importance of intimacy coordination has become increasingly apparent following high-profile developments of the #MeToo movement.

Creating a Framework of Action

Intimacy coordination not only establishes boundaries, but also lays out a framework within which the intimate activity occurs. As a scene is developed, the work is to discuss the intimate engagement of the material and arrange a framework of exactly what will happen. The scene is then rehearsed fully clothed. This preparation can appear quite matter of fact and terms used are anatomical and realistic. Unprepared movement improvisation is avoided, but once the sequence is created, there is room for spontaneity of expression within known steps of leading and following, all rehearsed into the action. Actors should feel safe, supported and respected when working through a sequence of events, such as the practical aspects of clothing removal in the scene, and be provided with appropriate body part coverings.

Discussion at All Points

Every stage of the work is discussed with the actor, with the director present, and crucially the performer can say what is comfortable or not. Feelings and reactions that may emerge for the actor regarding the sensitive and personal nature of the scenes can be voiced in rehearsal. Ita O'Brien here outlines the stages of collaborative work with the actors, which will involve:

- Meeting the actor and the initial talk about the script.
- Day of the shoot: planning the activity, establishing the acceptable or unacceptable.
- Rehearsing and deciding on the content, followed by discussion.
- Viewing of filmed footage at the end of the day.
- A post-shoot meeting.
- Follow-up discussion held a few weeks later or after the film is released.

WORKING IN FASHION

Movement directors have long collaborated in fashion image-making, but their role is expanding to advertising campaigns and promotions because of an increased use of images, not least the moving image. This field is being increasingly defined by mobile devices and social media, and how the technology is used for promotion and dissemination of content to commercial ends. In this context, a fast-moving and changing landscape has evolved that requires the skills of a movement director for the devising and composing of action for both still and moving images.

Cameron McMillan – Movement Director, Choreographer and Dancer
Creating for a Concept or Brand

Advertising companies come up with a concept and idea for garments or outfits and they have very clear objectives, because the shoot will produce the face of a brand for the next season. The work I produce as movement director is in a collaborative situation (with the client, art director, stylist and photographer) and fits into a big social and media construct. I think it is important to be socially, politically and culturally very aware of the impact of images in relation to the current trends. An explosion of content is now required by markets, brands and by individuals for self-promotion, driven by digital technology that offers a constantly changing flow of images.

The Campaign

A mood or style for the campaign is generated by the client's art direction and concept team. The aim of a shoot is, ultimately, to create a brand, promote and sell products, and it is important to understand the target market. As movement director, I create the action with the model or artist, which is then captured in the images. A shoot can be across one or two days. Preparation will mean working on the campaign concept from a mood board of images. It is about making creative and artistic choices around that, elevating the real world into something more – not just making material that is glossy. It also means thinking on your feet in relation to the references given.

Talent, Models and Artists

The models or artists can be drawn from different disciplines, as fashion campaigns open doors for very different types of artists and people from different types of movement backgrounds. As talent, they may have a big name in their field (theatre, music or dance) and a social media profile. In the highly visual, digital, online world of fashion, the media influence of wearers themselves, along with the fashion, has become increasingly significant. The clothes often lead the physicality because they need to be presented in a way that looks good. Sometimes movement is limited, or you are unable to do things that you might want to do because it's about working with the clothing or fabric, and how the body is captured in the image or footage. I think the traditional view of how bodies are represented is shifting, which means fresh ideas that are both challenging and exciting are being sought.

Translation

I offer terminology for people (photographers and video directors) who don't have a movement language or the words to communicate exactly what they want from the artists. They may want something very specific, so their ideas need to be translated on to the body for the artist or model, with whom I communicate directly. As a movement director, there are some very basic practices that I use, such as how their breath is used, how relaxed they are, where their focus is, and discuss the intention or thinking behind a move. I am the one who comes up with the movement material and in the process there is a search for authenticity in making the body and garments look good and that the action reflects the style and ambience required by the client. I check the shots or footage in the monitor to see how the material and action is composed and framed, and communicate directly with the photographer.

PHYSICAL COMEDY

Creating Humour

Physical comedy is essential to the world of theatre. To create humour, a set of skills is required of the movement director, which may include elements of mime and clowning – although as distinct art forms, they deserve their own book. The archetypal Fool, whether wise or comic, features importantly and in different guises appears throughout literature and play texts, and notably in Shakespeare. Samuel Beckett, pioneer of absurdist theatre, was interested in vaudeville and the comic, dry-faced entertainers who emerged from it. *Waiting for Godot* (1953), reflecting Samuel Beckett's love of the form, was revived with music hall comedian Max Wall in the cast. He had expert deadpan delivery, great physical skills, timing and a wicked engagement with the audience. The format of his one-man show had the same physical material each time, but he engaged with audience members (a latecomer, a non-laughing man and an old lady) in a way that took the show on a different trajectory each time.

Great Physical Performers

The performers associated with physical comedy, include artists Marcel Marceau, Max Wall, Charlie Chaplin, Karl Valentin, Buster Keaton, Lucille Ball, Laurel and Hardy, Jacques Tati and the Russian clown Oleg Popov. More recent comic performers from film and TV include Richard Prior, Julie Walters, Whoopi Goldberg, Peter Sellers and Michael Crawford. The legacy of the silent film genre and mime traditions is available in fragments on YouTube.

Jos Houben – Performer, Movement Director, Educator

Expertise in the Genre

Jos Houben, performer, movement director and Feldenkrais practitioner, spoke of the essentials and mysteries of comedy as part of theatre-making. Jos trained with Jacques Lecoq himself and was one of the founders of Theatre de Complicité. Our conversation revolved around the themes of what lies at the heart of the comedy and makes it come about. The questions brought rich and mercurial responses from Jos – a great movement artist and comedian himself. It is worth seeking out his work in *L'art de rire* (2010) and *L'art de jouer animal* (2017) available on YouTube.

In performer and movement training for theatre, it's important to provoke a way of thinking through action not merely about action.

Finding the Absurd

The great comedy performers of the past, such as in Music Hall or European vaudeville, included eccentric dancers or performers who developed skills for their acts. There was the man who grimaced, making ridiculous faces, or a woman who sang off-key, a quick-change artist, or a performer who sat behind a screen, breaking wind. These performers earned a living through an absurd type of comedy. In my practice I have sought to find the absurd. When I was asked once to take part in a devised comedy, I asked what it was to be about, and the reply was 'It doesn't matter'! That was great as I could pursue my fascination with the Dadaists and surrealism and how,

as art movements, they created a refusal to offer meaning. There was a throwing up in the air of all the prior codes of expectation and a new meaning was allowed to be born. That said, funny performers can truly create meaning and depth in their performance.

Comedy Deals with an Idea that We Anticipate

The more I learn about the complex and mysterious thing that movement is, the more I find that life is there. So, in general, we have a way of being in life that likes smooth, undulating lines or more than jagged lines, as in a sort of harmony rather than something staccato. We are in tune with what the expected 'right' movement or move will be – as can be found in watching the expertise of dance, football, music and so on. What we anticipate is generally well executed, fluent and somehow right, in how it achieves a result. Outside of that expected order, are moments that could be mis-timed, are too fast, too slow or interrupt that flow – like a hiccup or tripping over – and they cause humour. In short, if we sit watching a lake: it is calm, immovable; a fish jumps; it's a moment of delight with a sense of surprise – we laugh.

Movement and Space

The work of Jacques Lecoq was not only about the effect of movement on the spectator but, crucially, the effect of movement on the space. In all theatre-making, but especially in comedy, it is important to find ways that movement 'can create space around itself' and how movement affects the space around it and, of course, the audience.

Rules

In life, we can play by rules and obey them; thereby an excellent, totally right or ordered result occurs. Comedy is another way to play as it disobeys and breaks the rules, thereby achieving disorder, failure and laughter. In comedy performance there is always a flip side. Even in a tragedy or national disaster, we can find physical humour and deal with it through that.

How to Engineer Laughter?

I came across the work of, and met, Johnny Hutch (1913–2006). He was an acrobat, performer and expert in music hall routines, who had been working on the vaudeville circuit from a young age. At only five feet tall, he had worked in circus and became a TV actor in the Benny Hill show. He continued performing till he was 72 (he admitted that walking on his hands was harder with arthritic wrists) and taught acrobatics, routines and stagecraft in the latter part of his life. Through his experiences, he had a superb knowledge of all the music hall routines, chases, gags and manoeuvres.

Johnny Hutch used to say about comedy and the gags:

> It is the audience that will tell you if you've got it right or wrong. You do this (meaning a precise action) and they don't laugh. Adjust the timing. They laugh. It's all in the little moves.

Construction

I watched the comedy work in film clips of the great performers – Charlie Chaplin, Buster Keaton, The Marx Brothers and Jacques Tati – and developed a training in movement for comedy. I analysed their gags and routines by precisely reconstructing the action. By doing this, I found out a lot about the very necessary precision needed to make them work. We inspected, out of the context of the scene, the almost choreographic detail in the timing of any comic action. It's important to respect the precision in the construction, because if you are a beat too late, the laughter doesn't come. I really respected the tradition evolved by these great performers.

Jos Houben as Performer

A Minute too Late (2005) is a work of physical comedy, made with Simon McBurney, Marcello Magni and Annabel Arden. It was successful and toured the world. It dealt with simple and direct themes and offered movement as physical comedy that was beyond language and was ideal for the British Council theatre department to offer for a range of countries and cultures.

> I carry a thread from Lecoq and it's a creative thing – being taught by him and becoming part of a community of performers. We were taught to be creators and performers. Feldenkrais training was an essential part of my formation as a performer, and I also teach that.

Laurel and Hardy reconstruction.

CHAPTER 9

WORKING IN COLLABORATION

This chapter has been developed from conversations and working with directors David Lan, Brigid Larmour, Femi Elufowoju Jr and Matt Ryan. They have helped outline the communication and dialogue needed for collaborative theatre-making with a movement director.

THE CONTEXT

As introduced in earlier chapters, the professional context is a crucial part of the creative chemistry involved in the work of movement directors. In general, the director, having chosen their creative team, usually works most closely with the set designer to develop a concept for their approach to the work. Along with the lighting designer and other visual effects artists, the movement director is a significant player in the realization of the director's vision. Directors cast the performers, although the movement director is often, but not routinely, consulted about anyone who is required to have specialist dance or physical skills for a role.

The collaboration between the director and movement director begins from the first meeting about the play, develops through the exploration and shaping of ideas in the rehearsal room, and continues throughout technical rehearsals into performance. The movement director and director will work very closely with the same group of performers in the rehearsal room. There may, inevitably, be some cross-over in terms of approach, and both creatives will navigate the territory of rehearsal process in a range of ways.

For me, working with movement to release aspects of the play is crucial at the early stages of the process and gives an informative organic result, developed through the bodies of the actors.

Femi Elufowoju Jr, director, speaking in a master class, Doorway Project (2021)

Two Pairs of Eyes

The view of the action emerging can mean two pairs of eyes observing the actors through very different lenses. For example, the movement director will be focused on movement or dance, seeing the staging potential as a more abstract development of the action, but also with focus on the performers' skills in delivery of the movement. However, the director will be seeing the encounters in the action as stories unfolding between the characters, and the fuel that can offer for the play in its realization as a production. The actors' choices may reveal to both director and movement director the crucial character traits and interaction between characters that will become relevant within the world of the play. This dual vision is where understanding and mutual respect are significant.

The Director's Role

Directing involves establishing the situations, thoughts, intentions, emotions and development of characters with the performers in the framework of the script. These are among other almost invisible capacities and skills, such as leading the company and guiding the creative team.

Artistic director Brigid Larmour, suggests that directorial guidance and leadership with the actors are concerned with investigating the characters, and the many layers involved in a play and the story to be told by them. She observes that the skills of 'staging action' and 'directing' when working on a play are different and that some directors are stronger in one area more than the other.

> *Staging has to do with the action within the stage space, and the frame or geometry of action and this activity can often be shared with the movement director.*
>
> Brigid Larmour in conversation (spring 2021)

Some aspects of the director's role, such as the staging of scenes can, at times, be closer to those of a choreographer or movement specialist. In the studio, with the performers, the director as leader of a team can afford to be accepting of a movement director's intervention in the creative process. Ideally, the movement director is invited at different stages of the process, into a shared ebb and flow of discussion about the decisions and choices coming forth.

Imagination and Intuition

Working on a play, a director creates in a room where imagination and intuition are at play with the actors. David Lan, producer and director, suggests that there are some directors who instinctively make use of staging skills to create meaning in space and time within the theatre space, as a choreographer does when working in dance. He gives the example of Ivo van Hove, the renowned Dutch director, who works in a choreographic way. Van Hove recognizes the valuable skills of the movement director but can navigate his own process, including his own work on movement in the rehearsal studio.

> *...sometimes the process needs no other person present to distract or question the singular vision of the director and the work emerging with the actors...*
>
> David Lan

The Movement Director's Role

As introduced in earlier chapters, the skills and observations of the movement director focus on the movement of the actor's body, their physicality and its connection to character. Understanding of the actor's creative working process needs respect for details and clues, which they carry on the journey toward performance. Acknowledging the work shared between director and actor on intention, backstory and sub-text is vital.

The movement director can lead a full company warm-up, the creation of a common movement language for an entire ensemble, as well as specific skill development for individuals. A warm-up can include interactive games for the ensemble, although some directors don't like these, as they can give a wrong message if they are not targeted toward the theme and content of the play. The process includes generating style and group behaviour as physicality for the world of the play, or arranging dances mentioned in the script. The other important role may include creating scene changes to facilitate a seamless flow of action, essential to the narrative.

Working Together

Close collaboration presents a situation where creativity and intuition and personality can get all mixed up in the delivery of movement work that will inevitably become part of a single result. The movement director's offers, contributions as ideas within the whole, may well become subsumed as part of the final presentation, and some passages that they have created may even go under-recognized.

> *The work together is about being a director with movement and in effect, sliding between worlds in the creation process. When working*

with director John Tiffany, I am handing over 'the goods' to him as the director. What you have done in the process can happen quietly and often only the performers and the director know that you have been there at every key moment in creating the staging, to facilitate the emergence and realization of the ideas.

Steven Hoggett in conversation (2020)

Time

The movement director's time to work creatively in the studio needs negotiating and to be established before rehearsals start. It is the most often discussed issue and the most difficult area to negotiate – in some cases, this is time for creativity and development for the director as well as the performers and movement director. The problem of how much time is granted the movement director to develop material or to contribute lies, initially, in the hands of the producer. Time in terms of a finite length to the rehearsal period is also about money. Time needs to be managed as part of the budget and the schedule for the project. In the rehearsal room, is it a question that the director may have to relinquish time for script work and staging in order for equally productive movement work to be done with the company?

Navigating

Movement directors are integral to the collaborative team. It takes a relaxed and confident attitude toward the entire production for ideas to take life within the envelope of the directorial vision. Ideally, all contributions, from actors and movement director, will enhance and complement the final work. There is incredible creative potential, to have artists working at the top of their game in the sharing and bouncing of ideas, with the resulting richness coming from generous contributions and offers – and their acceptance.

RELATIONSHIP WITH ACTORS

It's very important to acknowledge, respect and appreciate the close-knit work that takes place between a director and the actors. The director's work with the actor will establish the intentions for a role in a process that continues from the beginning, through studio and technical rehearsals to performance and afterwards, in the form of notes as feedback.

The actor takes on board specialist input on voice and movement work, and consultation about costume and appearance. The director's relationship with the play and the actor is respected by everyone, so that conflicting information does not confuse the actor. The work on movement may well enlighten or serve to enable the actor to reach hitherto undiscovered aspects of a role. An overload of information is also a potential risk for the actor who will undoubtedly appreciate input but still must process ideas, observations and resources. It is worth remembering, as David Lan, director and producer, points out, that 'all of the work is happening within the same actor's body' and is carried by them into performance from the journey begun in the rehearsal room.

Professional Conduct

A vital element for the movement director in a collaborative working environment is keeping to one's role and not crossing boundaries inappropriately. In the vibrant ecology of a rehearsal room, emotions and psychological issues, such as confidence and insecurity, are present. The camaraderie of performing companies and post-rehearsal drinks can become a place of disclosure and complaint. Whatever the circumstances, it is wise not to share with any actor or performer:

- An alternative view of an intention that has been given by the director.
- Differences of opinion between you and the director.
- That there could be a better way to do the scene.
- Negative views on frustrations about the working process.
- Ideas that might compete with, or depart from, the initial brief.

HOW A MOVEMENT DIRECTOR IS SELECTED

For any project, the crucial choices for the director will be the collaborators for the creative team. Artistic director Brigid Larmour outlines what she might consider when selecting the right movement director for a new production and shows the thought that goes into creating a good rehearsal ambience.

- What background, experience and knowledge does this person bring with them?
- What sort of a character is that person? Would the project work creatively for them?
- What is the nature of the project – what are the tasks to be fulfilled and the skills required?
- What are the systems of training and thinking, which that person is immersed in, and do I understand them?
- As the director, what do I need in terms of movement? Is there any overlap between my own skills and understandings and theirs?
- Can this person work with the psychological impulse of the actor, as well as with the technical matter of bodies in space?
- What is their ability to work with the skill levels of a given company of performers?
- Are they good as a supportive, practical helper and companion to help climb the mountain?
- Do I need someone who can be provocative or different? How would this person stimulate a different approach from me?

Initial Meetings on a Project

The initial discussions with the director will inform about what their version of the production will be concerned with. Sometimes several meetings are needed to arrive at clear parameters of what will be appropriate and acceptable, and what could be off-limits as resources for the world of the project. Movement directors informally have voiced concerns when very little information is forthcoming from the director about the project. Conversely, if the outline or brief is overly specific it can be restrictive in terms of any creative offers made by the movement director. In both cases, it feels necessary to somehow almost get inside the director's head to achieve something that might work for them and the production, and that satisfies both creative imaginations. One crucial factor will be expectations and realities on either side concerning the rehearsal time needed to achieve or realize the movement work.

A First Meeting

Sometimes a meeting may not be so straightforward. About fifteen years ago, I asked for a meeting on the production I was engaged for. It was with a famous director who also ran a major theatre and was always very busy. The production had begun rehearsal, but the company manager suggested 'the company meet and greet drinks on Thursday' would be a good time. I sat down notebook out and fired off several questions, writing rapid (hopefully legible) notes on his responses. Then his PA arrived to say that a cab was outside waiting, with his wife and children. The meeting lasted ten minutes. We next met in the rehearsal room when I arrived at a call to start work. The scene to be resolved was a famous one in terms of movement, in a major Shakespeare revival.

Kate Flatt

SHARING THE FLOOR – NAVIGATING THE REHEARSAL PROCESS

The Director's Brief

Director Brigid Larmour suggests that the brief for the movement director is 'a two-way process' built out of discussion. For her, initial discussions will include 'how to be in the room together'. She aims to be very clear with the movement director as to what the expectations are and to discuss the use of rehearsal time. In forward-planning for rehearsals, she likes to give time for movement work, especially at the outset, although it may be important not to do too much at once. She considers the allocation of time that might be needed, and then is prepared to double that. If the aims in the brief are not possible in the overall scheme of the rehearsal period, then it is worth changing the expectations of what is achievable. She points out that the collaboration relationship will, of course, be tested in the rehearsal studio, but it is important to establish a working language together early in the process. In her process, she reputedly gives a good amount of time to the movement work. In her experience, some movement directors need a plan as a clear brief or description for the movement work. Others need a more open brief as a creative outlet and are comfortable in a fully collaborative situation.

Working as a Team

Creative collaborators on a theatre production work as a team and want to develop the material as best they can, by contributing to the result. Tastes, likes and dislikes will need to be shared between the director and movement director as respectful yet candid exchanges, toward the clarity, depth and richness desired and being found. It undeniably means that creatively, each needs to offer up and share ideas as a team process with any problem-solving that may emerge.

The movement director needs to make body knowledge available to the performer, so that the director can see results or transformation in the character development. The responses of the director to a section made by the movement director will need to acknowledge what is not working but allow space for the movement director to solve it. The movement director brings their specialist knowledge and toolkit for that purpose. Brigid Larmour suggests that both directors and movement directors generate meaningful action but there may be overlap in their individual ways of doing this. Both may envisage, develop and plan action from scratch. Rules and laws about what will work and make the material legible will depend, to an extent, on how a

story is embodied and the movement director can really help with that.

As a director, I need to have some distance to see the results of movement work and then can comment on it for further development.

Brigid Larmour

Establishing a Rapport

Collaborative studio engagement indicates a need for sensitivity, intuitive engagement, responsiveness and mutual respect for the unfolding work. It is in the beginning stages of a rehearsal process that the relationship between the director and movement specialist gets established. Finding rapport and understanding each other's process is key, because when the floor is shared, choices and decisions are coming from two observation points. It is not always possible to sense or gauge the reaction of whoever is working alongside you. The rehearsal studio with performers present, and on a tight schedule, does not offer much opportunity to discuss what is happening. It is difficult to quickly explain any reactions about your approach or view of the material. Mercifully, tea and lunch breaks enable time to reflect, observe and discuss tactics about the work

Holding – and Sharing – the Room

For emergent directors, importance is given to the concept of being able to 'hold the space'. This term is drawn from psychological or therapeutic situations and points toward everyone present feeling held and safe within the exchanges that take place. In theatre-making practice, the concept of 'holding the space' can be applied to the rehearsal studio and the performers engaged in development of the play with the director and collaborators.

The theatre rehearsal room can be a complex, multi-faceted environment for all concerned in which vulnerable aspects of all involved are present. With the performers, there can be fears of unexpected instructions or requests they may not know how to respond to, or sometimes individual, often private concerns relating to limitations to their skills, risk-taking or general confidence.

> *It's the director's responsibility to make a working space comfortable for the movement director, as it is also crucial to see how they solve problems, keep the show on track in rehearsal, and hear how they speak and interact in response to other collaborators.*
>
> *Director Matt Ryan in conversation (autumn 2020)*

A Safe Space

Rehearsal rooms and companies of performers benefit from a situation in which, throughout the entire rehearsal process:

- A 'safe space' enables everyone to contribute creatively.
- Play and exploration are possible and productive.
- Those leading can read the room and successfully manage activity in the room.
- Responsibilities for the developing work are shared.
- Value is given to the creative work of everyone in the room.

Experienced directors and performers will have learnt how to handle unknown and new situations, but younger less-experienced practitioners can find situations, such as day one of rehearsals on a new play, rather daunting. The director and movement director will need to read the room, to gauge the psychological temperature of the studio and its occupants. Once, being mindful of the actors assembled for the first day of rehearsal on a new production, director David Lan turned to me just before we walked into the studio and said, 'It's worth remembering that everyone in there is more afraid than you are'.

Questions arise in a collaborative situation if 'holding and sharing the room' is not a positive, creative experience:

- Do those present in the room feel that they are in a place of exploration, play and growth?
- Is it clear who is 'holding' the room at any one time?
- Are all enabled to contribute creatively and imaginatively to what is emerging?
- Are the boundaries for activity within the rehearsal made clear?

GOOD COLLABORATION

Any collaborative process requires an open mind, being generously supportive and accepting that it takes two to build a relationship. There are skills and

THE DIRECTOR'S BEST ASSET

Steven Hoggett, movement director for *The Curious Incident of the Dog in the Night-Time* (2012) and *Harry Potter and the Cursed Child* (2016) observes:

> *A movement director is the director's best asset. It means being seated in a rehearsal and watching, watching all the time, to find moments of release or physical understanding. There is the important task of leading in the making of movement sequences – possibly in another studio – then sharing that. The role entails being the constancy in the room throughout the production rehearsals for everyone. This can be by offering tools to play with or develop a character with or by stripping stuff away and sometimes by rebooting the material if it's got stuck somewhere. At times you need to lead [or pull] from the front [show leadership] and at others you need to push from the back [be supportive].*
>
> *Steven Hoggett, Movement Director, in conversation (2020)*

qualities essential for successful delivery of a single result, where shared imaginations have the potential to give form to ground-breaking theatre.

Rufus Norris, in a conversation at the National Choreographers Conference held by One Dance UK in 2013, suggested that 'collaboration and sharing the floor is not always an easy process and the job of the director can be demanding, tough and lonely'. He offered a summary about the creative partnership or team, outlining that there is a need to find yourself working alongside someone who:

- Has sensibilities, standards and taste that you can mutually trust.
- Has the understanding that when a moment offers up something promising, you can both jump on it and pursue the idea together – and let go of it again if needs be.
- Inhabits and shares the same emotional world view.
- Has no hesitation about stepping up to lead from the front, taking over if needed.
- Is a load-sharer, supporter and carrier of the emergent work.

Rufus Norris in conversation, Dance UK, National Choreographers Conference, YouTube (2013)

On to the Stage

Entering the theatre for stage rehearsals after a final studio run through, the rehearsed action needs to find its place as an entity within the theatre space. At this point, the director and team will feel the weight of responsibility for what the audience and

critics will see. It is a time of pressure, demand and challenges. If all goes well, the collaboration established in the studio will result in a sense of connection and communication created with the material for the audience. The discerning lens of the movement director is always about the movement but can also observe what occurs from a wider perspective, to help pinpoint a more interesting or viable way to realize a moment.

Gesture.

KEY CAPACITIES IN COLLABORATION

From *One Dance UK* (formerly *Dance UK*) *Magazine*, Autumn (2008):

Empathy The ability to understand and share another person's feelings and ideas, and to respond intuitively to the emergent premise and the resulting work. This quality helps the currency of the imagination to be well oiled, enabling a flow of ideas to deepen. It stops things getting stuck and releases the best in others.

Abrasion Asking the awkward question(s). This quality helps turn corners in an overly nice or over-empathized environment. It stems from a need for better guidance as to who is leading/following the train of thought. Like emery paper for striking matches, it can cause sparks and ignite the thinking process.

Listening Not second-guessing the other person or people, such as the director, another collaborator or the performers. Hearing more than speaking. Allowing a train of thought to reach its conclusion. Not interrupting is good manners. Asking a further question when appropriate: 'can you tell me more about…?'.

Sharing a viewpoint on the emergent material or work Offering an observation on what occurs. Giving flashes of insight, which occur in viewing the work in progress or what is occurring as the work unfolds. Pick your moment for that. An off the wall spur of the moment response can solve a problem, an entire act or the work as a whole. Trust it – share it – and relax if it seems not to bite or get taken up. Collaborators need thinking time.

Dogged pragmatism – logistical insights Viewing a challenge or problem in the cold light of day, especially during the pressure of stage rehearsals. Sorting out the nuts and bolts that make a 'vision', a moment or a transition work. Without killing an idea how can it realistically be made to work? What needs to adapt to make a specific flight of fancy become a reality without losing magic?

Yielding To the whole, toward ongoing work, to other ideas or crucially giving way if needed. Committing to the emergent results. Reflecting on what is important to the story and the creation of the whole. Not getting upset if an element you have contributed goes by the wayside.

Valuing Appreciating and acknowledging the ownership of the contributed ideas. It may be that by halfway into the working process no one even knows, remembers or cares where, how or when the best idea came up. It shouldn't matter. However, it is important to acknowledge all creative team members involved in the work that contributed insights as elements of authorship. The director's appreciation of the contribution to the result is vital.

Raising the game A constant process of searching to make stronger, more investigative choices by continuing to probe deeper, accepting what is going on but pushing the boundaries.

Working with performers This is about engaging with yet another group of collaborative relationships as these people (actors and performers) 'carry' the work of everyone. Their discoveries and contributions are inevitably shaping the work. Sensitivity to them, their expectations; how their relationship with the director is different yet inter-related. Help them to enhance their performance through notes, support and technical insights.

Life in the fast lane This is when a project is culminating, when the pressure is on because of the limits of technical time when problems may be occurring. Vital to retain respect for other collaborators; working with the team, listening and contributing but not forcing or driving; accepting if something doesn't work and making changes for the better. This period of production tests the best of temperaments and professionalism. Keeping objectivity is vital. As is keeping one's cool.

CONCLUSION

I hope that this book has revealed and clarified for readers the mysteries of the movement director's knowledge, craft and skill. In writing the book, I have found out a great deal about the practice and research of colleagues, as well as how we share a serious approach to imagination and creativity. Inspired by practitioners' insights, we can acknowledge confidently how the movement director's authorship has a distinct, very visible and significant place in the scheme of live theatre-making and opera production.

TEN THOUGHTS

For all those who aspire to create with movement for live theatre, these ten thoughts are, for me, an inherent part of theatre-making as a movement director.

1. Acknowledge and value your bodily knowledge and movement experience.

2. When time is short, use it wisely – it's finite not elastic.

3. Embrace and trust your intuitive judgement.

4. Be generous and supportive with performers and collaborators.

5. Be generous and supportive with offers and ideas. Accept they may not all be needed.

6. Research and preparation are vital, even if it is not all visibly used in a production.

7. If interpersonal difficulties in the work arise, then listen, understand and read the situation, before taking any action.

8. Emotions tend to run high in theatre-making, but people, like weather in the UK, are very changeable, and any bad bits, created by the situation, don't last.

9. Movement direction has intangible aspects, beyond words and rational explanation.

10. Whatever the process, the results will live in the hearts and minds of the audience.

PROFESSIONAL DEVELOPMENT, SUPPORT AND FURTHER STUDY

MOVEMENT DIRECTORS' ASSOCIATION

The UK Movement Directors' Association is an artist-led network formed in 2020 that celebrates the work of movement directors and elevates their voices. Our mission is to create better working conditions by promoting a deeper understanding of our contribution within the profession. We are connecting a thriving community and representing our collective artistic interests. Founded in 2020 by Ayse Tashkiran and Diane Alison Mitchell (https://www.movementdirectorsassociation.com).

Aims are to:

- Advocate for movement direction as a field.
- Increase the visibility of movement directors.
- Make space for movement directors to meet, share and grow.
- Improve standards and conditions for all movement directors.
- Act as a hub of resources and information about our craft.

Actions:

- Campaign for more equitable working conditions.
- Dialogue with industry bodies for recognition.
- Quantify the field through a comprehensive survey.
- Voice the movement community.
- Widen access to movement direction as a career path.

MOVESPACE

MoveSpace was founded in London in 2017 by Laura Dredger and Ingrid Mackinnon to support movement directors, teachers and practitioners, offering both free and affordable professional development opportunities to UK-based creatives. It has built a network of peers by facilitating conversations and events, opening discussions, opportunities and space for emerging and established movement practitioners to engage, share skills and exchange ideas. The role of a movement director can be solitary and has a feeling of isolation. MoveSpace continues to listen to the needs of its members, developing new programmes to support this growing industry. MoveSpace has been effective in offering support, guidance and reassurance during short- and long-term projects, through Space to Move (practical workshops) and Space to Talk (virtual/in-person meet-ups) initiatives (www.movespace.org.uk).

THE DOORWAY PROJECT

Conceived as a professional development intensive, the Doorway Project is designed for early- and mid-career directors, movement directors and choreographers to work with performers. All participants receive an honorarium, supported by public funding from the Arts Council of England. The Doorway Project offers opportunity for fresh discovery made through the live chemistry of collaborative exchange and discussion. As a paid opportunity, dancers, actors and a small group of directors and choreographers are selected to investigative creative strategies toward inter-disciplinary staging. Collaborative tasks offer ways to examine the source material through movement, space, rhythm and breath, toward non-literal ways of realizing scenes as a migratory journey between text and movement. Material created as vignettes, rather than complete scenes, are shared at a collective event at the end of the intensive, creative sessions. In a climate of product-driven creation, the project has been evaluated as having a significant impact on career development, the notion of 'time out' and the chance to refresh ideas through peer exchange.

The Doorway Project concept was initiated by Kate Flatt in 2003–04, together with director David Lan at the Young Vic, using as source texts *Blood Wedding* (1932) by Garcia Lorca and *As You Like It* (1599) by Shakespeare. In 2019, a second edition was developed with partners the Young Vic Directors' Program and Watford Palace Theatre. It was co-facilitated by Kate Flatt with director Brigid Larmour, with a focus on scenes from Shakespeare and, in 2021, with Femi Elufowoju Jr, using scenes from *Raisin in the Sun* (1959) by Lorraine Hansberry, *The Dybbuk* (1913–16) by S. Ansky and *Generations* (2005) by Debbie Tucker Green. Follow-up, open workshops were given for emerging practitioners at the Young Vic in 2019, also as part of their Directors' Program. Future Doorway Projects are planned from 2022, to enable introduction to collaborative working in opera and ways to employ shared, collaborative research, for movement in plays (www.kateflatt.com).

FURTHER STUDY

Movement studies form an important part of actor training in conservatoires and also in drama and performing arts courses at BA and MA level. The innovations of the well-established MA programme mentioned here have had a significant impact on the growth of the profession in the UK, Europe, USA, Latin America and Australia.

MA MFA Movement: Directing and Teaching at Royal Central School of Speech and Drama, University of London

These programmes of advanced study are for those who wish to consolidate their own practice and re-imagine their movement trainings for actors. The programmes, conceived by movement teachers Vanessa Ewan and Debbie Green, give subject status to the craft of actor movement within conservatoire settings. Movement director and teacher Ayse Tashkiran has co-led the programme with Vanessa Ewan since 2004. Originally entitled MA Movement Studies, the name change gives professional recognition to movement direction as a practice and highlights the importance of 'doing' movement, as well as thinking and articulating.

The part-time and 2-year MFA pathway enables further study by second career movement practitioners. Students include homegrown and international movement practitioners, which has led to the growth of graduate movement activity in Chile, Columbia, Mexico, Australia, China, the USA, Canada, Greece, Spain, Italy, Denmark, Norway and the Netherlands.

The programme offers time, space and support for students to question and investigate their movement heritages and body knowledge, and to re-imagine practice for actor training and movement directing. Students undertake a movement direction unit where they are supported and coached in discovering their unique creative engagement with narrative, and approaches to the dramaturgical and collaborative demands of movement direction. Students undertake placements within Central, other drama schools and universities, within opera and theatre companies, and applied theatre settings. The programme has a dynamic alumnus, whose ambassadorship manifests in teaching, directing and facilitation settings, as well as through doctoral study and artistic practice across theatre, film and television, opera and musicals. Their voices have fed back into the programme through mentorship, academic teaching and movement sessions. A full list of graduates can be found here:

https://www.cssd.ac.uk/courses/movement-directing-and-teaching-mamfa.

International Community for Movement

In 2014, the course leaders established the International Community for Movement to engage with the wider movement community through discussions and discoveries of movement teaching and directing (https://www.cssd.ac.uk/Teaching-at-Central/excellence-and-innovation-in-teaching/icm).

CONTRIBUTORS' BIOGRAPHIES

Vicki Amedume.

Lucy Cullingford.

Vicki Amedume has over 20 years of experience of working in circus, outdoor arts and theatre, following her initial training as a research scientist. She founded Upswing, a contemporary circus company, in 2006 following a career as a circus performer in the UK, France and the USA. An award-winning performance company, Upswing uses the human body as an expressive tool to entertain, inspire curiosity and ignite a desire to build connection. Vicki is an associate director at The New Vic in East London and an associate director at The Albany, Deptford. Beyond Upswing, she has provided circus and aerial direction within productions, to a range of companies including the RSC, the National Theatre of Scotland, the Royal Exchange Theatre and Kenny Wax Productions, as part of the creative team for the Olivier Award-winning *The Worst Witch*.

Lucy Cullingford is a choreographer and movement director working in theatre, opera, dance and film. She trained at The Northern School of Contemporary Dance, Bretton Hall College and has an MA in Movement Studies from The Royal Central School of Speech and Drama. Lucy was artist in residence on creative fellowships at both York and Warwick universities, and teaches across theatre disciplines, in all areas of the industry. Lucy was movement practitioner for RSC's inaugural movement department 2008–10, including work on the original *Matilda the Musical*. Recent credits include: *Death of England* and *All of Us* (National Theatre); *The Wizard of Oz* (Leeds Playhouse); *The Taming of The Shrew* and *Measure for Measure* (RSC); *Don Quixote* (RSC and West End); *King Lear* with Ian Mckellen (Chichester Theatre and West End); and *Constellations* (The Royal Court, West End, UK National tour, and Broadway).

Sarah Fahie is a director and movement director working in the UK and internationally. Born in Australia, she studied at the University of Melbourne and as a dancer at the London Contemporary

Sarah Fahie.

Jonathan Goddard.

Dance School. In 2003 she received a Jerwood Foundation Choreography Award. Movement direction credits include: *Peter Grimes* (La Scala, Milan); *Rodelinda* and *Don Giovanni* (English National Opera); *Der Rosenkavalier* (Glyndebourne Festival); *Don Giovanni* (Bergen National Opera); *Capriccio* (Grange Park Opera); *Hänsel und Gretel, Semele and The Skating Rink* (Garsington Opera); *Aida* (Royal Albert Hall); *La traviata* and *La bohème* (Opera Holland Park); *Don Giovanni* (Northern Ireland Opera); *The Gambler, Il tabarro, Suor Angelica, 4.48 Psychosis, La bohème, Kát'a Kabanová* (ROH); *The Trial* (Young Vic); *Endgame* (Old Vic). Future plans include: *The Valkyrie* (ENO) and *4/4* (ROH).

Jonathan Goddard is a dance artist, movement director and choreographer. His most recent performance work includes *The Mother,* a full evening duet with Natalia Osipova by Arthur Pita. He won the Critics Circle Award for best male dancer twice, in 2008 and 2014. Movement direction credits include: *Romeo and Juliet* (NT Lyttelton Films);

Anthony and Cleopatra, Strange Interlude, Man and Superman, Beaux Stratagem, As You Like It, Sunset at the Villa Thalia (National Theatre); *The Cherry Orchard* (Roundabout Theatre, Broadway); *Timon of Athens, Two Gentlemen of Verona* (Royal Shakespeare Company). Movement and research associate: *Matilda* (Working Title Films/Netflix); *West Side Story* (Leicester Curve). Dance associate: *Charlie and the Chocolate Factory* (Theatre Royal Drury Lane). His choreographer credits include: *While You Are Here* with Lily McLeish Company and *Chameleon's Pictures We Make* (Linbury Theatre).

Asha Jennings-Grant holds an MA in Movement Studies (Royal Central School of Speech and Drama) and a BA (Hons) in Dance Performance (Middlesex University). Following a career as a dancer, her movement direction work has been for theatre, dance, opera and motion capture for the past seven years. Credits include: *Shuck 'n' Jive* (Soho Theatre); *HONK!* (Trinity Laban); *Closer Than Close* (KYRA); *The Taming of the Shrew* (Arts Theatre, London);

Asha Jennings-Grant.

Joyce Henderson.

The Magna Carta Plays (Salisbury Playhouse); *PUSH* (The New Diorama Theatre); *Clemency* and *Noye's Fludde* (Union Chapel); *Machinal* (Rose Bruford) and *Watership Down* (Watford Palace Theatre). She has taught movement at the Royal Central School of Speech and Drama, Rose Bruford College, Mountview Academy of Theatre Arts and the Royal Welsh College of Music and Drama. She currently works with Pit Stop Productions as Physical Performance Director on video games.

Joyce Henderson trained with Jacques Lecoq in Paris. She is an associate of Complicité, appearing in *The Street of Crocodiles*, *The Magic Flute* and teaching projects locally and internationally. As a practitioner of movement, Joyce has contributed to productions in theatre, opera, dance and film. Recent projects include: *Noises Off* (West End); *The Marriage of Figaro* (Aix Festival); *Crave* (with Julie Cunningham and Company, Barbican); and *The Midwich Cuckoos* with Sky TV. Joyce assisted on the Opening Ceremony of the Olympic Games in 2012 and has also assisted Deborah

Warner on productions including: *Julius Caesar* (Barbican and international tour); *Dido and Aeneas* (Vienna, Amsterdam and Paris); *Between Worlds* (Barbican); and *King Lear* (Old Vic).

Steven Hoggett is an international choreographer, director and movement director. Steven's credits include West End and National Theatre productions *The Ocean at the End of the Lane*, *The Light Princess*, *Pinocchio* and *Black Watch* (National Theatre of Scotland). Steven was co-founder of Frantic Assembly with whom he created over twenty shows, including: *Peepshow*, *Othello*, *Beautiful Burnout*, *Lovesong*, *Stockholm* and *Little Dogs*. Broadway credits include: *Harry Potter and the Cursed Child*, *Angels in America*, *The Crucible*, *Curious Incident of the Dog in the Night-Time*, *The Last Ship*, *Rocky*, *The Glass Menagerie* and *Once*. At the Metropolitan Opera his work includes *Rigoletto*. Steven's work with recording artists includes: David Byrne, Tori Amos, Burt Bacharach, Green Day, Sting, Nico Muhly, Imogen Heap, Phillip Glass and Olafur Arnalds. Music video collaboration

Steven Hoggett.

Jos Houben.

includes: Bright Light, Goldfrapp, Franz Ferdinand and Bat for Lashes; and film includes: *Freak Show* (Maven Pictures) and *How to Train Your Dragon* (Dreamworks).

Jozef (Jos) Houben (b. Bruxelles 1959) is internationally acclaimed as an artist in comedy, physical theatre and music theatre. Performing, writing, teaching and directing worldwide for the past thirty years, he has worked with many leading international organizations and artists, such as: Peter Brook, Simon McBurney, The National Theatre London and L'Opera Comique de Paris.

Since 2000, Jos has worked as a teacher at the École Internationale Jacques Lecoq in Paris. He is a Feldenkrais practitioner and also teaches master classes throughout the world at international festivals, circus and theatre schools, and universities. His hit, one-man show, *The Art of Laughter*, has travelled the world for the last fifteen years.

Brigid Larmour is artistic director and chief executive of Watford Palace Theatre. Her interests include: nurturing new artistic talent, new writing;

making classic texts passionate and accessible; promoting cultural diversity and gender equality, which speaks to, and represents, the widest possible community. Brigid is a producer, director, dramaturg and teacher with experience in subsidized and commercial theatre and television. Credits at Watford Palace include: *Much Ado About Nothing* by William Shakespeare; Dodie Smith's *I Capture the Castle* adapted by Teresa Howard and Steven Edis; *Arms and the Man* by Bernard Shaw; *Coming Up* by Neil D'Souza; *Jefferson's Garden* by Timberlake Wertenbaker (Best New Play 2015); Laurence Marks' and Maurice Gran's *Love Me Do* (co-directed with Shona Morris) and *Von Ribbentrop's Watch*; *Fourteen* by Gurpreet Kaur Bhatti; Gary Owen's *Perfect Match*; *Mrs Reynolds and the Ruffian*; Ronald Harwood's *Equally Divided*; Charlotte Keatley's *Our Father* and *My Mother Said I Never Should*; and pantomimes by Andrew Pollard: *Aladdin*, *Dick Whittington*, *Sleeping Beauty* (co-directed with Shona Morris*)*, *Robin Hood* and *Mother Goose*.

Brigid Larmour.

Ingrid Mackinnon.

Ingrid Mackinnon is a London-based movement director, choreographer, teacher and dancer. Her movement direction credits include: *Romeo and Juliet* (Regent's Park OAT); *Josephine* (Theatre Royal Bath/ The Egg); *Hamlet* (RCSSD); *Bonnie & Clyde* (London College of Music); *The Merchant of Venice* (RSC First Encounters); *Typical* (Nouveau Riche, Soho Theatre); *Liar Heretic Thief* (Lyric); *Reimagining Cacophony* (Almeida); *#WeAreArrested* (RSC and Arcola); *The Border* (Theatre Centre); *#DR@CULA!* (RCSSD); *Kingdom Come* (RSC); *Fantastic Mr Fox* (associate movement Nuffield Southampton and National/International tour). Ingrid has taught dance technique for London Contemporary Dance School and London Studio Centre, and is a visiting lecturer teaching actor movement at Guildhall, Mountview, ALRA South and RCSSD. Ingrid is co-founder of MoveSpace and holds an MA in Movement: Directing & Teaching from the Royal Central School of Speech and Drama.

Cameron McMillan is a choreographer, dance artist and movement director. He has an international performance and creative career spanning contemporary dance, ballet, film, the fashion and commercial fields. New Zealand born and raised, he

Cameron McMillan.

was a dancer with Rambert Dance Company and English National Ballet, and with several companies in Australia and New Zealand. As a choreographer, he has been commissioned by festivals and companies in America, Europe and Australasia. Cameron was artist in residence at the Hong Kong Academy for Performing Arts (2017), associate artist with Dance East (2010–14) and rehearsal director for UK company Ballet Boyz. Alongside work for the stage, he brings choreographic skills to inform the way both still and moving image is created, in collaboration with photographers, visual artists and directors. Clients and publications include: *REDValentino*, *Lacoste*, *Adidas Originals*, *Pepe Jeans*, *Garage Magazine*, *POP*, *Pleasure Garden Magazine*, *L'Officiel Paris*, *Pan and The Dream*, *The Last Magazine*, *Muse Magazine*, *Office Magazine* and *Twin*.

Sasha Milevic Davies works as a movement director, choreographer, director and dramaturg. She was a founding member and artistic associate of the Yard Theatre, and was part of Festival d'Avignon's, Voyages de Kadmos programme for emerging artists. Awards include Muci Draškic Award for Best Director

Sacha Milevic Davies.

(Constellations/Moja Ti). Credits include, as director: *The Language of Kindness* (UK Tour); *She Ventures and He Wins* (The Young Vic); *Pet Života Pretužnog Milutina*, *Moja Ti*, *Constellations* (Atelje 212, Serbia). As movement director: *Pity*, *Shoe Lady* (the Royal Court); *Touching the Void* (Duke of York's Theatre); *Antipodes* (National Theatre); *Our Town* (Regent's Park Open Air); and *Berberian Sound Studio* (Donmar Warehouse). As choreographer: *Everything That Rises Must Dance* (Complicité/Dance Umbrella); *The Halt Yozgat Murder* (Staatstheater Hannover); *The Merry Wives of Windsor* (The Globe); *The Writer* (Almeida); and *The Suppliant Women* (Royal Lyceum, Edinburgh/ATC/Young Vic).

Diane Alison Mitchell is a movement director, theatre choreographer and actor movement tutor who trained at the Central School of Speech and Drama. She is head of movement at Guildhall School of Music and Drama and was part of the creative team for the London 2012 Olympic Opening Ceremony. Recent theatre credits include: *When The Crows Visit*, *Wife*, *Holy Sh!t* (Kiln Theatre); *A Midsummer Night's Dream* (Criterion Theatre); *Shuck 'n' Jive* (Soho Theatre); *Our Lady of Kibeho* (Royal & Derngate/Theatre Royal Stratford East); *The Hoes* (Hampstead Theatre); *They Drink It In The Congo* (Almeida Theatre); *SOUL* (Royal & Derngate/Hackney Empire); *Othello*, *Julius Caesar* (RSC); *The Emperor Jones* (LOST Theatre); *How Nigeria Became: A story, and a spear that didn't work* (Unicorn Theatre); *The Gershwin's Porgy and Bess* (Regent's Park Open Air Theatre); *We Are Proud to Present a Presentation about the Herero of Nambia* (Bush Theatre); *The Island* (Young Vic), *Lola – The Life of Lola Montez* (Trestle Theatre); and *The Relapse* (Embassy Theatre).

Anna Morrissey studied archaeology and anthropology and went on to train in dance and movement at the Royal Central School of Speech and Drama. She has worked as movement director and choreographer at major UK venues and internationally. She worked on the London 2012 Olympic Opening Ceremony and has been commissioned to make dance works by the ROH and Historic Royal Palaces, as artist in residence. Credits include: *The Winter's Tale* (RSC); *Translations* (National Theatre); *Emilia* (Shakespeare's Globe, West End, Olivier Nominated Best Comedy); *Imperium* (West End, RSC); *Swive* (Shakespeare's Globe); *Queen Anne* (West End); *Richard III* (Almeida Theatre); and *King Charles III*

Diane Alison Mitchell.

Anna Morrissey.

(West End, Almeida Theatre, UK tour, Broadway). Opera credits include: *Current Rising* (Linbury Theatre, ROH); *Amadigi* (Garsington); *The Turn of the Screw* (ROH); *Swanhunter* (ROH, Opera North); and *Macbeth* (NI Opera/WNO).

Jenny Ogilvie Following early dance training, Jenny studied modern languages then trained and worked as an actor for ten years. She then brought together her experience as a performer and her love of movement, and completed an MA in Movement Studies at the Royal Central School of Speech and Drama. She works as a director and movement specialist on theatre and opera productions in the UK and internationally, and movement direction credits include: *The Marriage of Figaro*, *Cunning Little Vixen* (English National Opera); *B* (Royal Court); *A Midsummer Night's Dream* (Young Vic); *Hobson's Choice* (Royal Exchange Manchester); *Greek* (Scottish Opera); *Midsummer* (National Theatre of Scotland, Edinburgh Festival); *Rutherford and Son*

(Sheffield Crucible); *Plenty*, *Crave* (Chichester Festival Theatre). Internationally she has worked at Vienna State Opera on the world premiere of *Orlando*, and at Opera Wuppertal, Hannover State Opera and Brooklyn Academy of Music, New York.

Ita O'Brien is the UK's leading intimacy coordinator and founder of Intimacy on Set, her company set up in 2018, which provides services to TV, film and theatre when dealing with intimacy, sexual content and nudity. O'Brien pioneered the role of the intimacy coordinator and since 2014 has been developing best practice Intimacy on Set Guidelines, which have been widely adopted in the industry advocating for safe, fair and dignified work for everyone. O'Brien has worked on numerous high-profile productions including: *Normal People* (BBC3/Hulu); *Sex Education 1&2* (Netflix); *Gangs of London* (Sky Atlantic); *The Great* (Hulu); *I May Destroy You* (BBC/HBO); *Brave New World* (Peacock/Sky One); *It's A Sin* (Channel 4); and has been widely covered in

Jenny Ogilvie.

Ita O'Brien.

the national and international media as the leading spokesperson in this space.

Ayse Tashkiran is a movement director, teacher and researcher. She read drama at Bristol University and trained with Lecoq in Paris. Ayse has led MA MFA Movement: Directing and Teaching at Royal Central School of Speech and Drama since 2004, and is an associate artist at the Royal Shakespeare Company.

Credits include: *Europeana* (Projekt Europa); *Shakespeare in Love* (National Tour); *Othello* (Sam Wanamaker at the Globe); *Fantastic Mr Fox* (Nuffield Theatre); *The Government Inspector* (Birmingham Repertory Theatre); *York Minster Mystery Plays* (York Minster).

For the RSC: *As You Like It*, *The Provoked Wife*, *Romeo and Juliet*, *The Duchess of Malfi*, *Doctor Faustus*, *Hecuba*, *The Shoemaker's Holiday*, *The White Devil*, *The Merry Wives of Windsor*, *Richard III*, *King John* and *Measure for Measure*.

Publications include: *Movement Directors in Contemporary Theatre: Conversations on Craft* (Methuen, 2020); *The Actor and his Body* by Litz Pisk, new introduction by Ayse Tashkiran (Methuen 2017); 'British Movement Directors' in *The Routledge Companion to Jacques Lecoq*, ed. by Rick Kemp and Mark Evans (Routledge, 2016).

Ayse Tashkiran.

GLOSSARY

Auteur A term associated with film, but also used in relation to theatre direction, it is someone who as director articulates the world of the film, play or opera, asserting a very personal, recognizable style and subjective view on the source text or scenario.

Beats These denote a way of breaking down and analysing longer sections of a script into more specific, shorter chunks or sections as recognizable shifts in action or thoughts. A 'beat' is a dynamic shift and can last for as long as a topic is being discussed or an exchange takes place. If a new character enters or if all characters change topic, then a new beat begins.

Biomechanics This is the study of movement in relation to function and mechanisms of the skeleton and muscles. It was developed by Meyerhold in Russia, as a systematic, technical approach to movement and an alternative to the psychological and intention-focused activity of Stanislavsky's theatre.

Blocking The performers' moves in a play or opera, which give a framework and structure for the action. Instructions in use refer to action in the space, such as '...move directly to stage right', 'moving upstage', '...make a banana', 'break to downstage left' and so on.

Body-Mind Centering Developed by Bonnie Bainbridge Cohen, BMC offers a set of principles as an approach to movement, touch and learning, applied by people involved in many areas of dance and movement arts, including bodywork, somatic movement, dance and psychotherapy.

bpm The measurement of beats per minute used for Italian musical tempi terms and speeds. Using a metronome, we can identify Largo – Slow as 40–60bpm, whereas Presto – Fast is 160bpm.

Choreographer Literally a writer of dance movement. A choreographer writes with movement to create dance, just as a photographer creates with light to capture images.

Contract A formal letter of agreement or legally binding contract between an employer or contractor and artist as employee, which lays out the terms of engagement, pay, dates, managerial aspects, job title and other aspects of the work to be undertaken.

Devised Theatre Works of theatre based on a concept or idea that starts without a script. The work is explored through contributions by all concerned in the creation process, from collective voices, in the collaborative task of creating a complete entity, overseen by a director. Examples include, in the UK, the work of Frantic Assembly and Theatre de Complicité.

Dumbshow The definition from the Oxford English Dictionary suggests 'Gestures used to convey a meaning or message without speech'. It also refers to a sequence of wordless movement or action, as mime within a play, which serves to summarize or comment. In *Hamlet*, the 'play within a play' has a dumbshow as part of it.

Foley This is the art of how sound is produced for a film soundtrack. It was used as a live onstage device in several productions of Katie Mitchell's *The Waves* (2006) and *Some Trace of Her* (2011) at the National Theatre. The actors made the sound effects live on stage, in a production that included mixed media and live video feed.

Galen (c. AD129–216) He was an Ancient Greek physician, surgeon and philosopher who influenced the development and understanding of anatomy, physiology, pathology and healing. He developed the concept of the four humours and that of *pneuma* – breath.

Intention Is the thought or motivation behind any action, or simply 'why' something happens. It becomes intrinsic to the action, rather than something added on or acted out superficially. Intention is embodied in movement, visible or felt, both in the actual vocabulary of the material and how it is communicated.

Jig A dance known to a wide sector of the Elizabethan population. A jig continues to form a feature in the Globe Theatre productions and is danced by the ensemble to close performances of Shakespeare's plays to this day. The jig is still found in various forms in Britain and Ireland. The music encompasses a wide range of tunes in 12/8, 9/8 and 6/8 rhythms. Jigs still found in the Bampton Morris tradition in Oxfordshire include Fool's jig, Bacca pipes jig as well as Double jigs, a competitive form danced by two people.

Kinesphere A spatial concept of movement teaching and creation as defined by Rudolf von Laban. It refers to a 'sphere of movement surrounding the body, which can be reached by extending the limbs without changing one's stance' (from *Dance Words* by Valerie Preston Dunlop 1966).

Krump A freestyle dance genre from the USA. It is danced in competitive 'battle' sessions rather than on stage. Krump is different stylistically from other hip-hop dance styles such as breakdancing, although they share street origins, freestyle nature and the use of battling. Krump is danced upright to fast-paced music. It uses challenges but does not promote aggression or fighting.

#MeToo This is a term referring to sexual harassment and sexual assault, initially with reference to women in the film and theatre industries. It became used as a term on social media in 2006, by sexual harassment survivor and activist Tarana Burke.

Raked Stage This term refers to the steepness or slope of the stage, where the back of the stage is raised higher than the front of the stage. It was once used to create the illusion of perspective. Steeply

raked sets are quite common in contemporary opera design.

Rhetorical Gesture The art of gesture as allied to oratory and developed as a form in Roman times by Quintillian and Cicero. In theatre history, in the book *Chirologia . . . Chironomia* (1644) by James Bulwer, the emphasis in the illustrations is on hand gesture, as used in the Elizabethan Theatre, and the distinction between natural expression and rhetorical action. Advice on its use is given for both actors and orators.

Sense Memory In acting theory, the recalling of a prior experience in life is used to inhabit a character more fully on stage. For example, an actor might use sense memory to reconstruct a funeral or other event so that they are momentarily sad in recalling, for example, the sound of the rain or smell of the earth.

Slow Motion From film and as a cinematic aspect of time; the action appears to have been slowed down, giving a heightened sense of the action.

Staccato In music performance this refers to the quality of how each note is separated sharply from others and means detached in Italian. It contrasts with the quality *legato*, meaning smoothly flowing and literally tied or without breaks.

Staging For directors and movement directors this involves the activity of performers in the stage space, with the geometry and timing of it. It implies meaningful arrangement and structured presentation pertinent to a play, opera or musical. It may involve, but is distinct from, choreography. The term 'musical staging' refers to a choreographic approach in how sung material is shaped for an ensemble.

Text-Based Theatre Applies to all works that are scripted from the outset by a playwright and developed for performance by a director and creative team.

Vaudeville Stage entertainment as a variety show of short acts: slapstick, song-and-dance routines, comedy, acrobatics, etc. by duo and solo performers.

Voice-Over Actors' voices added as audio track to a film and, in animation, a character voice working with the movement of the character.

FURTHER READING

These books and articles are all ones I have found valuable to support my practice and feed into ways of nourishing imagination, feeling and movement work with performers in rehearsal situations.

Bullwer, John, *Chirologia: or the Natural Language of the Hand. Chironomia or the Art of Manual Rhetoric* (Thomas Harper, 1644)

Bachelard, Gaston, *The Poetics of Space* (Orion Press, 1964)

Bicat, T. and Baldwin, C. (eds), *Devised and Collaborative Theatre* (Crowood Press, 2002)

Bogart, A., *What's the Story. Essays About Art Theatre and Storytelling* (Routledge, 2014)

Bogart, A. and Landau, T., *The Viewpoints Book: A Practical Guide to Viewpoints and Composition* (Theatre Communications Group, 2006)

Brissenden, A., *Shakespeare and the Dance* (Dance Books Ltd, 2001)

Cave, R. and Worth, L. (eds), *Ninette De Valois, Adventurous Traditionalist* (Dance Books Ltd, 2012)

Cools, Guy, *Imaginative Bodies, Dialogues in Performance Practices* (Antennae Arts, 2016)

Evans, Mark, *Performance, Movement, and the Body* (Red Globe Press, 2019)

Ewan, V. and Green, D., *Actor Movement* (Bloomsbury, 2015)

Jarret Macauley, D., *Shakespeare, Race and Performance* (Taylor and Francis, 2016)

Lambranzi, Gregorio, *New and Curious School of Theatrical Dancing* (Dover, 2002)

Lecoq, Jacques, *Theatre of Movement and Gesture* (Routledge, 2006)

Leiter, S., *The Art of Kabuki* (Dover Edition, 1999)

Mitchell, K., *The Director's Craft* (Taylor Francis, 2008)

Nachmanovitch, S., *Free Play – Improvisation in Life and Art* (Penguin, 1990)

National Theater USA, *A New Practical Guide to Rhetorical Gesture and Action* (53rd State Press, 2018)

Newlove, Jean, *Laban for Actors and Dancers* (Nick Hern Books, 2001)

Nicholls, C., *Body, Breath and Being: A New Guide to the Alexander Technique* (D&B Pub., 2014)

Pallasmaa, J., *The Eyes of the Skin* (Wiley, 2007)

Pisk, Litz, *The Actor and his Body* (Methuen Drama, Bloomsbury, 2017)

Robinson, K. and Aronica, L., *The Element: How Finding Your Passion Changes Everything* (Penguin Books, 2009)

Rodenburg, Patsy, *Presence* (Penguin Books, 2009)

Rudlin, J., *Commedia Dell'Arte* (Routledge, London, 2004)

Sachs, C., *World History of the Dance* (W. W. Norton & Co., 1st edn 1963)

Stanislavsky, C., *Building a Character* (Methuen, 1990)

Taplin, O., *Greek Tragedy in Action* (Routledge 1993).

Tarkovsky, Andrei, *Sculpting in Time* (University of Texas Press, 1989)

Tashkiran, A., *Movement Directors in Contemporary Theatre: Conversations on Craft* (Methuen, 2020)

Thoinot, Arbeau, *Orchesography*, trans, C Beaumont (Dance Horizons, 1925)

Tufnell, Miranda, *The Widening Field, Journeys in Body and Imagination* (Dance Books Ltd, 2004)

Tufnell, Miranda, *When I Open my Eyes* (Dance Books Ltd, 2017)

Wesley, John, 'Original Gesture: Hand Eloquence on the Early Modern Stage', *Shakespeare Bulletin* (Vol. 35, 2017)

Whitley, Ann, *Look before you Leap. An Advices and Rights Guide* (One Dance UK, 2012)

Worsley, V., *Feldenkrais for Actors* (Nick Hern Books, 2014)

Zumthor, P., *Atmospheres* (Birkhauser, Basel, 2005)

INDEX